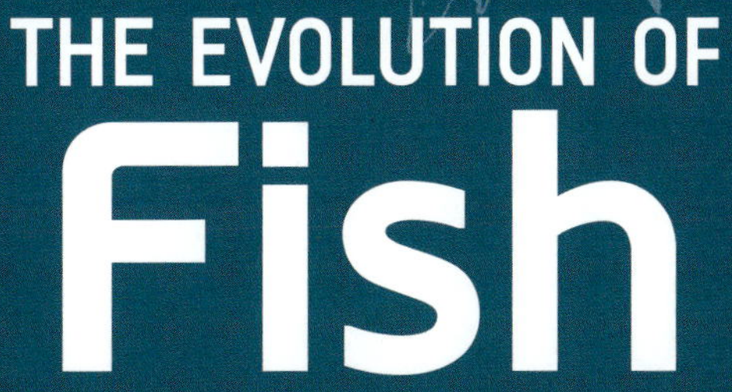

THE EVOLUTION OF Fish

by Carol Hand

Content Consultant
Dr. W. Leo Smith
Biodiversity Institute and Department of Ecology and Evolutionary Biology
University of Kansas

Essential Library
An Imprint of Abdo Publishing | abdobooks.com

ANIMAL EVOLUTION

abdobooks.com

Published by Abdo Publishing, a division of ABDO, PO Box 398166, Minneapolis, Minnesota 55439.

Printed in the United States of America, North Mankato, Minnesota.
092018
012019

Cover Photo: Grigorev Mikhail/Shutterstock Images
Interior Photos: L. Newman & A. Flowers/Science Source, 4–5; iStockphoto, 8, 14–15, 17, 25, 26–27, 36–37, 42, 50–51, 56, 64, 67, 70–71, 74, 76, 80, 87, 88, 90, 97, 99; Christian Darkin/Science Source, 11; Jacana/Science Source, 18; Shutterstock Images, 19, 41, 54, 65, 85; Pascal Goetgheluck/Science Source, 22; NOAA Office of Ocean Exploration and Research/Science Source, 31; Mark Kostich/iStockphoto, 33; Victor Habbick Visions/Science Source, 39; De Agostini Picture Library/Science Source, 45; Joy Lee/The Philadelphia Inquirer/AP Images, 46; Millard H. Sharp/Science Source, 48–49; Steven R. Smith/Shutterstock Images, 53; Blue Ring Media/Shutterstock, 58; Mark Smith/Science Source, 60–61; Tom McHugh/Science Source, 68; Neil Bromhall/Shutterstock Images, 72; Christian Jegou/Publiphoto/Science Source, 83; Jessica Merrill/iStockphoto, 93

Editor: Susan E. Hamen
Series Designer: Becky Daum

Library of Congress Control Number: 2018947967

Publisher's Cataloging-in-Publication Data

Names: Hand, Carol, author.
Title: The evolution of fish / by Carol Hand.
Description: Minneapolis, Minnesota : Abdo Publishing, 2019 | Series: Animal evolution | Includes online resources and index.
Identifiers: ISBN 9781532116643 (lib. bdg.) | ISBN 9781532159480 (ebook)
Subjects: LCSH: Fishes--Evolution--Juvenile literature. | Animal evolution--Juvenile literature. | Biological evolution--Juvenile literature. | Fishes--Juvenile literature.
Classification: DDC 574.30--dc23

CONTENTS

The Burgess Shale in British Columbia contains the best record of animal fossils from the Cambrian period.

CHAPTER ONE

From Fish to Tetrapods

Metaspriggina walcotti was an unimpressive-looking fish, except for its large, bulging eyes. It had no obvious fins and looked more wormlike than fishlike. It measured only 2.4 inches (6 cm) long, so its life in the ancient oceans was hazardous.[1] It shared the ocean with gigantic predators such as *Anomalocaris*, a 6-foot (1.8 m) insect-like creature with sharp teeth.[2]

But *Metaspriggina* was a fast swimmer, and its seven pairs of gills provided plenty of oxygen to keep its energy high. It also boasted an exciting new evolutionary development. It had a notochord—a flexible rod extending the length of its body that provided support and a place for its strong bands of muscle to attach. That is, the notochord was an internal skeleton. This unassuming little fish lived 518 million years ago (MYA) in the ocean waters covering what is now British Columbia, Canada. It is the oldest fish now known. *Metaspriggina*, or something similar, was the ancestor of all of today's vertebrates—not just fish but also tetrapods.

COMPREHENDING GEOLOGIC TIME

A typical human family might produce four generations in a century. But with a lifespan of a single century, it can be difficult for a human to truly comprehend the stretch of time since fish first appeared on Earth. Fossils indicate *Metaspriggina* appeared 518 MYA; newspaper headlines often rounded this number to 500 MYA. But the difference in the two dates is 18 million years, not 18 years. During that amount of time, a human family would produce 720,000 additional generations.

More than 100 fossils of *Metaspriggina* were collected in 2014 from the Burgess Shale rock formation in British Columbia. These represent a breakthrough in scientists' understanding of fish origins. The fossils show several traits found in humans' vertebrate ancestors—a notochord, paired eyes, and gill arches, which are stiff structures that support the gills. These fish were also involved in the transition from filter feeding to developing jaws for feeding. The fossils show impressions of the fish's internal organs, including the heart, liver, intestine, and blood vessels. *Metaspriggina*'s notochord and dorsal nerve cord establish it as the earliest known member of the phylum Chordata, called a chordate. The dorsal nerve cord is the forerunner of the spinal cord. It runs the length of the body, along the top.

The first pair of *Metaspriggina*'s gill arches is highly developed, hinting at the later evolution of the jaw. This fish lacks bony vertebrae, the series of small bones making up the vertebral column, or spine. Thus, it is not a vertebrate itself, but it is definitely an ancestor to vertebrates. According to paleontologist Simon Conway Morris of Cambridge University, "in many ways this is the most exciting find . . . because it fills a really important gap in our knowledge of early chordate evolution."[3] Morris and paleontologist Jean-Bernard Caron of the Royal Ontario Museum collaborated on the 2014 study of this ancestral fish's fossils.

FISHY TERMINOLOGY

The word *fish* is a common term, not a scientific one. Like *worms*, *fish* refers to a variety of different animal types. For example, not all fish are bony vertebrates. Jawless fish and sharks have skeletons made of cartilage, not bone. Scientists use the word *fish* to describe one or more members of a single fish species. Twenty bluegills form a group of fish. But scientists would describe the various species of minnows, bluegills, basses, and catfish living in a pond as *fishes*.

Fossils allow paleontologists to learn about species of fish and other animals that lived millions of years ago.

THE RISE OF FISH

The fish fossil record is sparse, particularly for species without bones. Their fossils, like those of *Metaspriggina*, consist of impressions left in mud or sand. Over time, the fish's organic matter was replaced by minerals from its surroundings. Some impressions are well preserved, with easily visible structures. But even bony fossils are hard to come by. Fish fossils date back as far as 518 million years. Many are buried forever on the ocean bottom. Accessible ones are on freshwater lake bottoms and in rock formations from which oceans have receded or which have been pushed up as mountains formed. Fossilization is rare; finding fossils is even rarer. But paleontologists are persistent and continue to uncover new fossils.

PRIMITIVE VS. ADVANCED

Cladograms are branching diagrams that show the evolutionary relationships among groups of organisms. They show ancestors on the left and the various groups descending from those ancestors on the right. Some people assume the leftmost groups of a cladogram are simple and primitive, while the rightmost are specialized and advanced. They see evolution as a steady march of improvement toward an advanced form. This is not true. First, there are no scientific definitions for "primitive" or "advanced." These are not objective, measurable terms. Second, every group on the tree, regardless of location, is specialized to fit its own environment. Hagfish are on the far left of most fish phylogenies because they are oldest, not because they are simple or primitive.

Nodes on a cladogram are points where two or more groups of organisms diverge from each other. Nodes represent common ancestors of the organisms in the branching groups. The groups connected by any node can be flipped from left to right and remain correct. The tree only shows relationships. It does not define one group as more primitive or advanced than others.

Early fish ancestors obtained oxygen through their skin. They used their gill slits for filter feeding, a process of straining food particles out of the water. But as vertebrates became larger, they needed more oxygen. The large surface area of gills enabled them to increase their oxygen uptake, and gills became more important for respiration than for feeding. Jawless fish originated far back in the Cambrian period, more than 500 MYA, and dominated the oceans for over 200 million years. Only two types, hagfish and lampreys, remain today. Other early fish included the now-extinct placoderms, or armored fish, which had both jaws and protective armor. Placoderms evolved during the Silurian period, about 420 MYA, but were extinct by about 360 MYA, possibly because their heavy armor slowed them down.

A major advance in fish evolution was the rise of jawed fish with paired fins beginning about 425 MYA. These pairs of pectoral and pelvic fins correspond to the forelimbs and hind limbs, or arms and legs, of tetrapods. Paired fins improved fishes' speed and mobility. Jaws let them bite, greatly increasing their food choices. In addition, developing jaws led to the separation of respiration and feeding. Fish no longer had to suck in water to obtain food. This enabled them to become true predators. Spiny sharks were one important group of jawed fish. They lacked heavy head armor and thus were much faster than the earlier placoderms. They appeared around 450 MYA and became extinct about 275 MYA.

The *Arandaspis* prehistoric fish lived about 500 MYA and was a precursor to true bony fish.

The two most important groups of modern fish evolved from different ancestors. Both first appeared in the fossil record about 210 MYA. Sharks and rays have skeletons made of cartilage rather than bone. Ray-finned fish have bony skeletons and other unique characteristics, including fins composed of webs of skin supported by bony spines.

A separate group, the lobe-finned fish, was most diverse between about 419 and 298 MYA, during the Devonian and Carboniferous periods. A few of these species still exist today. Lobe-fins are especially important because they were the ancestors of all the rest of today's vertebrates, the tetrapods. That is, the common ancestor of amphibians, reptiles, birds, and mammals was a lobe-finned fish.

Of the six fish groups that have appeared and spread throughout the oceans in the more than 500 million years since *Metaspriggina* lived, two groups—placoderms and spiny sharks—are now extinct. Another two—jawless fish and lobe-finned fish—have declined to only a few families. Today, ray-finned fish and sharks and rays dominate the oceans.

HOW EVOLUTION WORKS

Evolution can most simply be summarized as descent with modification. Over many generations, the descendants of a common ancestor begin to diverge from the ancestor. In the short term—a few generations—populations might show different color patterns or responses to environmental temperatures. When populations are separated for many generations, they eventually change so much that they form new species.

Changes in the genetic composition of populations and species over time result from natural selection, a process first described by Charles Darwin in 1859. Natural selection requires two conditions: genetic variation and selective pressure. The differences within a population caused by individuals' genetic variation, or differences in their genes, provides the raw material on which natural selection acts. Selective pressure is outside pressure from other organisms or environmental forces that affects whether an individual can survive. It can be positive or negative; that is, it can increase or decrease that organism's chances of survival. The result is differential reproduction: organisms with one form of a trait reproduce more successfully and leave more offspring than those with other forms. For example, suppose a fish species shows variation in fin size and that the fish with larger fins are more agile. More large-finned fish avoid predators and reproduce. They have more offspring than fish with smaller fins, and their offspring inherit the large-finned trait. Over time, the percentage of large-finned fish in the population increases. In natural selection, the more favorable trait eventually dominates.

Evolution by natural selection has led to an astonishing diversity of fish species in the world's oceans, brackish environments, and fresh waters. More than 30,000 species, representing more than 95 percent of all existing fish species, are bony fish.[4] There are another 1,259 species of cartilaginous fish, 123 species of jawless fish, and only eight species of lobe-finned fish.[5]

THE IMPORTANCE OF JAWS

Fish that developed jaws could catch bigger, faster prey than their ancestors because their mouths were larger and opened wider. The face was a key to vertebrate evolution. A fossil from China of a fish that lived 419 million years ago has the same cheek and jaw structure as today's vertebrates. This fish, *Entelognathus primordialis*, had cheeks plus jaws with a mandible and maxilla shaped much like these bones in humans. It was unlike other members of its family, the placoderms. Their simple cheeks and jaws had only a few large bones. *Entelognathus*, like today's bony fish, had smaller bones with more complex arrangements.

Lampreys, which have round, jawless mouths, have evolved little over millions of years.

CHAPTER TWO

Hagfish and Lampreys

Jawless fish, also called cyclostomes (meaning "round mouth"), belong to superclass Agnatha. Today, this superclass contains two classes of living fish groups—hagfish and lampreys. It is the most ancient group of living fish and the earliest group of vertebrates. Agnathans differ from other vertebrates in several ways. They do not have hinged upper and lower jaws. Instead, their mouths are circular and unhinged. They have not evolved paired fins or limbs. They have cartilaginous rather than bony skeletons. Some extinct agnathans had bony, protective armor plates under their skin, mostly around the head. Today's agnathans lack this armor.

HAGFISH AND LAMPREYS

Approximately 81 species of hagfish still survive in cold regions of today's oceans.[1] They have long, eel-like bodies and two rows of sharp teeth surrounding their circular mouths. They use these teeth to burrow into dead carcasses or sometimes live prey. To deter predators, they can produce massive amounts of a sticky, bitter, slimy protein that fills the predator's mouth while the hagfish slides away. Today, some hagfish are threatened by fishing and accidental capture. One species is classified as critically endangered, two species as endangered, and six as vulnerable.[2]

Forty-five species of lampreys still exist.[3] Lampreys breed only once in their lives and then die. Some species live their whole lives in freshwater. In other species, adults live in oceans but swim up rivers to breed in freshwater. Their young go through a several-year stage as larvae in freshwater. These larvae, called ammocoetes, burrow into sand or silt in stream bottoms, where they feed on algae and debris. Then they go through a metamorphosis and migrate to the ocean. Some species of metamorphosing lampreys develop eyes and a sucker-like mouth filled with sharp teeth. Once in the ocean, these species become parasites, attaching to larger fish and feeding on their blood and tissues.

CLASSIFICATION

Atlantic Hagfish
Myxine glutinosa

DOMAIN	**Eukaryota**. This domain includes plants, animals, and fungi. These organisms are grouped together because their cells each have a nucleus, a cell structure that contains the DNA.
KINGDOM	**Animalia**. All animals, including mammals and insects, are in this group.
PHYLUM	**Chordata**. Organisms in this phylum have a nerve cord down their backs supported by a rod of cartilage at some point in life. All animals with spines, including mammals and fish, are in this group.
CLASS	**Myxini**. This class contains jawless fishes.
ORDER	**Myxiniformes**. Hagfish, which live on the seafloor and feed on dead or dying animals, make up this order.
FAMILY	**Myxinidae**. Like the order, this family is made of hagfish.
GENUS	***Myxine***. Only one species is in this genus.
SPECIES	***glutinosa***. The Atlantic hagfish produces slime, which they expel when threatened, making it hard for predators to grasp the hagfish.

Taxonomic classification is the science of identifying living things, grouping them together, and naming them. When this is done, each organism is assigned a place in eight different categories ranging from domain, the most general category, to species, the most specific category. When the scientific name of an animal is given, it includes the genus, which is capitalized, and the species, which is not. The Atlantic hagfish is *Myxine glutinosa*. Scientific names are often abbreviated after first use: *M. glutinosa*.

LAMPREYS AS PESTS

Lampreys may be among the most ancient relics of our vertebrate ancestry, but that doesn't mean people like them. The sea lamprey was accidentally introduced into Lake Ontario more than 100 years ago and has spread into all five Great Lakes. After completing their larval stages, the fish remain in the lakes, where they become parasites on predators and game fish, including lake trout, lake whitefish, lake herring, and chub. Many parasitized fish either bleed to death or die of infections. Lampreys hate the smell of their own dead, so researchers hope to isolate a chemical from dead lampreys that will serve as a lamprey repellent.

Hagfish and lampreys have lateral-line systems. The lateral line is a sensory system that helps fish detect vibrations and pressure changes in the water. It uses receptor cells called neuromasts. Some neuromasts are embedded in the base of mucus-filled canals that run the length of the fish on both sides. When hair-like cilia in the neuromast are stimulated, they help the fish determine the direction and rate of water movement. This helps it keep track of its own movement and that of surrounding organisms. Other neuromasts lie on the surface of the fish. These make it possible for fish to determine the speed of the water in which they are swimming. This helps them maintain their position and is critical for keeping schools of fish together.

An artist's depiction of how a *Pikaia* may have looked during the Cambrian period

THE EARLIEST FISH

About 530 MYA, during the Cambrian period, the first fishlike chordates appeared. *Pikaia* was wormlike but had some key features of chordates. These features included distinct head and tail ends, bilateral symmetry, V-shaped bands of muscle, and a dorsal nerve cord. Its nerve cord was not protected by a spine of either cartilage or bone, so tiny *Pikaia* was a chordate but not a vertebrate.

Haikouichthys was only one inch (2.5 cm) long, but it had the beginnings of fins along its top and bottom.[4] Some consider it to be the earliest vertebrate and the earliest jawless fish. However, like *Pikaia*, it lacked a spine. A third noteworthy animal from the Cambrian period was

Myllokunmingia, which had gills located in pouches. Both *Haikouichthys* and *Myllokunmingia* were discovered in China in 1999. These fish may have had skulls made of cartilage, although this is not certain. Before these discoveries, the oldest known fishlike fossil was *Arandaspis prionotolepis*, which dated to the Ordovician period, 480 MYA. This species was similar to many fossil hagfish. It was jawless, lacked fins, and had armored plates covering its body.

Although earlier organisms such as *Metaspriggina* are fish, or at least early fish ancestors, they do not look very similar to today's fish. The most ancient fossils definitely identifiable as fish are the hagfish. The few fossils available are from the Carboniferous period, 330 MYA. They look similar to modern hagfish. Three fossil lampreys from the same time period have been found. Another, discovered in 2006, is from the Devonian period, 360 MYA. Lamprey fossils have a notochord with neural arches, which are a part of vertebrae.

With so few fossils to study, it is difficult for paleontologists to put together the evolutionary

THE EARLIEST CRANIATE?

Fossils from the Cambrian period, approximately 500 MYA, are so ancient that it is hard to tell if they were fish or even vertebrates. *Haikouichthys* was a tiny organism—only about one inch (2.5 cm) long.[5] It had a fishlike shape and was one of the first animals with a skull. It had several typical vertebrate features: distinct head and tail regions, bilateral symmetry, paired eyes, and a mouth on its head end. But was *Haikouichthys* really a vertebrate? So far, it is unclear whether it had a notochord or a spine.

history of cartilaginous vertebrates. These non-bony organisms do not produce as many or as well-preserved fossils as bony fish do. The timeline of chordate and vertebrate evolution will continue to shift as more fossils are found.

OSTRACODERMS

The Cambrian explosion was the sudden appearance of fossils with hard, bony skeletons containing calcium and phosphorus. It began about 542 MYA and was a major advance that may have led directly to the evolution of vertebrates. Exoskeletons, or external skeletons, came first. The oceans and freshwaters of the Ordovician and Silurian periods, from 490 to 410 MYA, were dominated not by vertebrates but by arthropods. These included giant sea scorpions approximately 6.5 feet (2 m) in length.[6] One group of jawless fish evolved a way to protect themselves from these predators. The ostracoderms evolved bone armor plating that covered their heads and sometimes their entire bodies. Two important ostracoderms from the Ordovician period were *Astraspis* and *Arandaspis*. Both were approximately six inches (15 cm) long.[7] They looked like big tadpoles, with large heads and no fins. They lived in shallow waters, bottom-feeding on tiny organisms and organic waste. Their descendants in the Silurian period were similar but had forked tail fins, which made them better swimmers.

In 2009, French paleontologists discovered a fossil fish head containing the oldest fossil brain discovered at the time. It belonged to a fish that lived 300 MYA.

The largest ostracoderms reached no more than two feet (60 cm) in length.[8] They had single median fins. Median fins are unpaired fins along the central plane of the body. They include dorsal, caudal, and anal fins. One group, Cephalaspidomorpha, may also have had paired lateral fins. Their gills were in pouches. Because of the heavy armor plating on their heads, more ostracoderms have survived as fossils than cartilaginous jawless fish. It is even possible to see the structure of their brains, nerves, and blood vessels. Fossils also show a pair of tubes at right angles to the fish's vertical, or top-to-bottom, plane. When filled with liquid, these tubes would have served as a balance organ, enabling the fish to be aware of its position in the water.

Ostracoderms lasted for several hundred million years. They were most diverse from about 425 to 375 MYA, during the Silurian and Devonian periods. In addition to their other vertebrate characteristics, they showed an advance in breathing that carried over into later vertebrates. They used their gills exclusively for breathing, not eating. They had separate gill pouches along both sides of their heads. But the gills were permanently open, lacking the protective coverings of modern bony fish.

Ostracoderms had efficient protection. But like other jawless fish, they were no match for fish with jaws. Their diversity began to decline about 400 MYA, and they became extinct by the end of the Devonian period, about 360 MYA.

THE MYSTERIOUS CONODONT

In ancient oceans, 500 to 250 MYA, conodonts were extremely common. Conodont fossils were first discovered in the 1830s by Russian paleontologist Christian Pander. They are small and shelled, with many sharp spikes protruding from them. They occur on every continent, and there are hundreds of kinds. For 150 years, no one knew what they were. Then, in the 1980s, a paleontologist at the University of Edinburgh discovered a slab of rock containing the complete impression of a lamprey-like organism. Embedded at its head end was a conodont. Conodonts were actually the teeth of ancient, jawless lampreys. Or, more correctly, conodonts were ancient lampreys whose teeth, but nothing else, were preserved. The reason there are so many conodonts and so few complete lamprey fossils is simple: the lamprey's body is soft, and its teeth are hard. Evolutionary reasons for development of the first hard parts—teeth, jaws, and armor—are simple, too. Teeth allowed animals to eat flesh instead of just sucking in organic matter. As larger predators evolved teeth and later jaws, smaller prey evolved hard armor for protection. This led to an evolutionary arms race in the oceans, centered around these hard body parts.

Paired Fins

Fish fins are used in swimming, including steering and forward motion. In some species they are also used for display, protection, sensing, and reproduction. Paired appendages are a key feature of all vertebrates. Fish have paired fins, and tetrapods have paired limbs—arms, legs, and wings.

Scientists continue to debate how paired fins evolved and eventually developed into paired tetrapod limbs. Some scientists think they evolved from gill arches that supported the gills. Others think they evolved from an ancestral median fin that completely encircled ancient fish.

A 2006 University of Florida study on spotted catsharks showed that the development of median fins in these sharks was controlled by the same genes that control human limb development. The same cell types produce median fins, vertebrae, and paired fins. Lampreys, which have dorsal and tail fins but lack paired fins, show the presence of the same genetic cues. This suggests the median fin genes first developed more than 500 MYA. The genes first produced unpaired fins, and about 100 million years later, paired fins. It was 200 million years before paired limbs appeared in vertebrates.

Stingrays can be found in warm, shallow tropical and subtropical waters.

CHAPTER THREE

Sharks, Skates, and Rays

There are 1,204 known species of sharks, skates, and rays.[1] Almost all sharks, skates, and rays are ocean-dwelling animals. These fish belong to the class Chondrichthyes and the subclass Elasmobranchii. Skates and rays together are sometimes referred to as batoids. Another small subclass, Holocephali, contains one group of 55 species of deep-water fish—the chimaeras.[2]

Chondrichthyes are gnathostomes, or jawed vertebrates, as are more than 99 percent of all modern vertebrates.[3] The basic gnathostome body plan includes jaws, teeth, and paired appendages. Gnathostomes arose from a common ancestor that separated at least 423 MYA into two lineages: the Chondrichthyes, or cartilaginous fish, and the Osteichthyes, or bony fish. A group of bony fish later gave rise to tetrapods.

CHARACTERISTICS OF CHONDRICHTHYES

All Chondrichthyes are vertebrates, with skeletons made not of bone but of strong, flexible cartilage. Cartilage in chondrichthyans is strengthened with many tiny prisms containing the mineral hydroxyapatite—the same calcium-based mineral that strengthens bone. Chondrichthyes also have jaws, paired fins, and paired nostrils. Their mouths are usually terminal or subterminal; that is, the mouth is at the very front end or slightly below it. But the mouths of skates and rays, which typically feed on the ocean bottom, are ventral, completely hidden under the body. The upper jaws of

SKATES VS. STINGRAYS

Skates and stingrays have several differences. Skates have pelvic fins with two lobes. Stingrays' pelvic fins have one lobe. Skates have relatively thick tails, and many have bucklers—large, thorny scales along the back and tail. Stingray tails are long and whip-like, with a stinging spine halfway along their length, but they lack bucklers. Most skates have two small dorsal fins and a smaller tail fin. Most stingrays lack dorsal and tail fins; a few have a small dorsal fin near the base of the tail.

Chondrichthyes are not fused to the cranium. This means their upper and lower jaws can move independently, giving them an extremely powerful bite. They have five to seven gill slits on the sides of their heads.

Chondrichthyan senses are highly developed. For example, they feel changes in electricity around them. Sharks use this electrical sense for hunting prey, for navigating through the water, and in social and mating behaviors. It helps make them skillful hunters and top predators. Sharks' lateral-line system enables them to detect prey from a distance of up to 820 feet (250 m).[4] Chondrichthyan fish lack swim bladders, which are structures used by bony fish to help them remain neutrally buoyant.

DO SHARKS DIE IF THEY STOP SWIMMING?

All sharks breathe by passing water over their gills. But this action works differently in some species. Species such as nurse sharks breathe by buccal pumping. They use mouth muscles to actively pull water into their mouths and over the gills. They can remain still, and they often lie in groups on the ocean floor. Other sharks use ram ventilation. They get oxygen by swimming very rapidly with their mouths open. The tiger shark can switch between ram ventilation and buccal pumping. But some sharks, such as great whites and makos, have lost the anatomy for buccal pumping. They would die if they stopped swimming.

Constant swimming does keep all sharks from sinking. Sharks lack swim bladders, the air-filled sacs used by bony fish to maintain neutral buoyancy, the balance between floating and sinking. Because sharks cannot maintain neutral buoyancy, they use their large pectoral fins to gain lift in the water, similar to how an airplane uses its wings to gain lift in the air. Sharks also have oil-filled livers that add buoyancy. Sharks can move to any depth, but if they stop swimming, they sink to the bottom.

Chondrichthyes have a heterocercal tail fin. This means the tail fin's upper lobe is larger than the lower one, and the fish's spine extends into the upper lobe. Finally, they have placoid scales, also called dermal denticles—literally meaning "skin teeth." These surface scales are composed of the same materials as teeth. As the fish grows, it develops more scales. Dermal denticles occur in regular patterns. In fast-moving sharks, the movement of water over the denticles helps them swim better.

TYPES OF CHONDRICHTHYES

There are approximately 538 shark species.[5] In addition to the features they share with Chondrichthyes, sharks have several unique characteristics. They have many rows of teeth that are constantly replaced throughout life. Their eyes are on the sides of their heads and are larger in deep-water sharks. Although they vary in size and shape, most sharks have rounded bodies that taper at the head and tail ends. This body shape makes most of them fast, efficient swimmers. Sharks have five types of fins—paired pectoral and pelvic fins, a single tail fin with a larger upper lobe, one or two dorsal fins, and sometimes a single anal fin. Fins help sharks swim and stay stable in the water.

The long-nosed chimaera has a paddle-shaped snout that has numerous nerve endings. These help the fish find prey.

Most of the approximately 669 species of batoids—skates, rays, and related species—live on the seafloor, often burrowing into the sand.[6] Batoids are flat, diamond-shaped animals with long tails. On top of their heads, they have eyes for viewing predators. Their gill openings are on the sides. They also have spiracles, openings that let them pump water over the gills without sand getting in. Their mouths are on the bottom, making it easier to capture bottom-dwelling prey such as shellfish.

The subclass Holocephali includes the chimaeras. Approximately 55 species of chimaeras live in deep ocean waters.[7] Chimaeras have four gill slits and large heads with big eyes and

SHARKS' TEETH

Some sharks have long, thin teeth for catching small fish. Others have wider, serrated teeth for catching and biting chunks out of larger prey. Unlike human teeth, shark teeth do not fit in sockets but are attached to the jaw by soft tissue. Sharks' teeth grow in rows. Several rows of replacement teeth constantly grow behind the functional teeth. Some sharks lose up to 30,000 teeth in their lifetimes. As teeth break off or get stuck in prey, new ones are always ready to replace them.

a snout. They move through the water by flapping their large pectoral fins. Instead of shark-like teeth, they have grinding tooth plates. The chimaera's body surface is covered with lines that look like seams, resembling Greek mythology's chimaera, a creature that is composed of multiple different animals joined together. Different chimaera groups are sometimes referred to as ratfish, rabbitfish, and elephant fish.

FOSSIL SHARKS

Entire shark fossils are rare because their cartilaginous skeletons do not preserve well. Most of scientists' knowledge of early sharks comes from isolated fossils of teeth and scales. The oldest scales date from 480 MYA, in the Devonian period, and some incomplete fossils are around 400 million years old. One of these is a Canadian fossil named *Doliodus*. Another, from 380 MYA, is the Australian fossil *Gogoselachus lynbeazleyae*.

A great white shark tooth sits atop a fossilized Megalodon shark tooth, demonstrating the size of the extinct shark that lived more than 2.6 MYA.

Found in 2005, this specimen included teeth, scales, lower jaws, shoulder bones, and pieces of gill arch. Because it had bone cells within its cartilage skeleton, it helped scientists understand that shark evolution is more complex than previously thought.

Most of the earliest shark fossils are from Australia and Antarctica. According to paleontologist John Long, this suggests sharks may have evolved in the Southern Hemisphere.

The oldest shark braincase is 380 million years old and is from New South Wales, Australia. In Antarctica, geologist Gavin Young found a partly connected shark skeleton, which he named *Antarctilamna*. The shark was small, only 16 inches (40 cm) long, and was probably the same species as the shark whose braincase was found in New South Wales. Both lived in freshwater. Both may have been xenacanths, prehistoric sharks with long, eel-like bodies for swimming through lake vegetation. But they had fin spines with thorn-like denticles, which were characteristic of the more shark-shaped ctenacanths. So far, too little fossil evidence is available to be sure of these earliest sharks' ancestry.

Paleontologists have only fossil teeth and scales, so they have no idea what most ancient sharks looked like. But teeth give clues about animals' lifestyles and evolution. Red Hill, an important fossil site in Pennsylvania, has extensive fossils from the Devonian period,

SHARKS WITH BONES

In 2005, paleontologist John Long of Flinders University in Australia found a 380-million-year-old fossil shark, *Gogoselachus lynbeazleyae*. Scientists once considered sharks more primitive than bony fish because they never developed bones. But the jaws of this ancient shark skeleton contain bone cells. This made it the first shark known to have bone cells binding the cartilage together. The shark appears to have evolved from an ancestor that had much more bone. According to Long, "The reason sharks are so successful today is because they've reduced the bone in their skeleton and become more lightweight with an entirely cartilaginous skeleton."[8]

including the largest known collection of fossil teeth of the shark *Ageleodus pectinatus*. A study of 382 teeth of this species indicated that Devonian teeth, like modern shark teeth, showed little wear. Thus, even ancient sharks could apparently replace teeth rapidly.

Cladoselache is the best-known Devonian shark because of some well-preserved fossils found in Ohio's Cleveland Shale region. *Cladoselache* resembles modern sharks, with a streamlined body, large pectoral fins, two large dorsal fins, and an upturned tail fin. But, like many Devonian sharks, its head was different. Compared to modern sharks, it had a long mouth and a weak jaw joint. Also, it lacked the solid vertebral column of modern sharks.

The number of shark species increased and spread throughout the Devonian and into the Carboniferous periods. Holocephali, the chimaeras, branched off in the Carboniferous period. Then, Chondrichthyes decreased until the Cretaceous and Tertiary periods, when their numbers began to expand again. Since the first sharks appeared more than 450 MYA, Earth has gone through five mass extinctions. Sharks have survived all five. They have adapted and diversified into many species throughout the world, maintaining the same highly successful body type. The last major changes, beginning about 200 MYA in the Jurassic and Cretaceous periods, resulted in the evolution of modern sharks. Today, sharks and their relatives are second only to bony fish in terms of abundance and diversity.

CHAPTER FOUR

Lobe-Finned Fish and Tetrapods

Many scientists have identified characteristics in living coelacanths that are not shared with other living fish. These show early steps in the evolution from fish to four-legged animals.

Earth's largest group of fish are members of the class Osteichthyes, or bony fish. Osteichthyes, in turn, is divided into two subclasses: Actinopterygii, or ray-finned fish, and Sarcopterygii, or lobe-finned fish. Sarcopterygii is unusual in a very important way. It contains two groups of living fish, the coelacanths and lungfish. It also contains all tetrapods, including humans. Because scientists now know that Tetrapoda evolved from lobe-finned fish ancestors, they have expanded the group to include

WHY FISH ARE NOT A CLADE

A clade is a phylogenetic group of species that contains a common ancestor and all of its descendants, like a family tree. It seems logical that all fish would form a clade, but they do not. The Sarcopterygii, the lineage that includes lobe-finned fish, also contains tetrapods. These are the vertebrates, a group consisting of amphibians, reptiles, birds, and mammals, including humans. Because this branch of the fish tree includes nonfish, or tetrapods, fish do not form a clade.

not only these fish, but also all tetrapods. Sarcopterygii is the only fish clade that contains nonfish.

Most sarcopterygians alive today are tetrapods and land dwellers. Few species are left in the two fish groups, although many more existed in the past. There are two surviving species of coelacanths, both in the genus *Latimeria*. These large deep-sea fish were thought to be extinct until a single specimen was found in 1938. The Dipnoi, or lungfish, consist of six living species in three genera.[1]

CHARACTERISTICS OF LOBE-FINNED FISH

The fleshy pelvic and pectoral fins of lobe-finned fish have a central region containing many bones and muscles. These fins make the fish very flexible. Two groups, lungfish and tetrapods, have adapted this characteristic to support their bodies on land. The paired pelvic fins join by

An artist depicted *Tiktaalik roseae*, an extinct lobe-finned fish that lived during the late Devonian period, using its fins to pull itself out of the water.

DISCOVERING COELACANTHS

In December 1938, Hendrick Goosen, a fishing captain in the Indian Ocean, caught a strange-looking fish. The specimen was described by ichthyologist, or fish scientist, J. L. B. Smith. He named it *Latimeria chalumnae* after Marjorie Courtenay-Latimer, a local museum curator who looked at the specimen with him. It was a lobe-finned fish called a coelacanth, a group of fish that was thought to have gone extinct with the dinosaurs about 65 MYA. In the late 1990s, a second coelacanth species, *Latimeria menadoensis*, was discovered in Indonesia. Some scientists assumed the coelacanth could be the closest relative of all tetrapods. In 1981, morphological studies by Donn Rosen and colleagues at the American Museum of Natural History showed lungfish were more closely related to tetrapods than coelacanths. And in 2013, an international research team sequenced the coelacanth's genome, or complete set of genes. This genetic study verified that lungfish, not coelacanths, are tetrapods' closest relatives and shared a common ancestor.

a single bone with the pelvic girdle, which is also called the hip girdle. The paired pectoral fins join to the pectoral, or shoulder, girdle with another single bone. When a group of lobe-finned fish gave rise to tetrapods, the single connecting pelvic bone became the femur, or hip bone. The connecting pectoral bone became the humerus, or upper arm bone. Lobe-finned fish have two separate dorsal fins; ray-finned fish have only one.

Coelacanths live in the ocean at depths up to 2,300 feet (700 m). They can reach 6.5 feet (2 m) in length and weigh up to 200 pounds (90 kg).[2] One species lives in the western Indian Ocean off the Comoros Archipelago in southern Africa, and the other lives in Indonesia. Coelacanths have ancient characteristics not

A fossil of a coelacanth on sandstone offers scientists clues about lobe-finned fish.

present in other living fish: a hinged skull that swings the cranium upward to enlarge the mouth, a hollow fluid-filled notochord, incomplete vertebrae, an oil-filled swim bladder, lobed fins supported by bone, and paired fins using the same synchronized "walking" movement as tetrapods. They also have a rostral organ, a gel-filled cavity in the snout that is connected by canals to the outside. It helps the coelacanth find prey by sensing electrical activity. However, its rostral organ is simpler and likely less important than the same organ in Chondrichthyes.

The six species of lungfish all live in freshwater—one in Australia, one in South America, and four in Africa. Their plate-like teeth crush and grind food. Their tail fin merges with the dorsal and anal fins. They lack bones that form much of the upper jaw in other fish. Lungfish often live in swamps and ponds that dry up for part of the year. During this dry season, they remain in the dried mud and breathe air. The swim bladder is modified as a lung. It is a pocket of the digestive system with many blood vessels. A lungfish gulps air and stores it, bringing oxygen into the

Lungfish are at home in the water and out.

blood as it runs through the lung. While lungfish still use gills in the water, the modification of swim bladders into lungs enables them to survive dry spells.

WHAT THE FOSSILS SAY

Fossils of lobe-finned fish have been found on all continents. The oldest fossils come from the early Devonian period, beginning about 419 MYA. By the end of this period, about 359 MYA, all major groups were present. Early lobe-fins were rapid swimmers. They had heterocercal, or asymmetrical, tail fins that were larger on top. Many living lobe-fins have symmetrical tails that are diphycercal; that is, their vertebral column extends to the tip of the tail.

Sometime during the early Devonian period, lobe-fins diverged into coelacanths and rhipidistians. Coelacanths remained in the oceans and flourished during the late Devonian and Carboniferous periods, through about 298 MYA, when they began to decline. Rhipidistians left the oceans and invaded freshwater habitats. They probably lived in shallow seas near river mouths. They also split into two groups, the lungfish and the tetrapodomorphs. Lungfish evolved the beginnings of lungs and limbs, enabling them to move over land to find new water sources. Tetrapodomorphs remained in water until the late Devonian, eventually evolving into tetrapods.

The earliest fish ancestors had gills, but lungs also arose very early in evolution. The common ancestor of lobe-finned and ray-finned fish had both lungs and gills. Early lobe-finned fish kept both organs, and today's lungfish and coelacanths still have both. Ray-finned fish retained gills, but their lungs eventually evolved into the swim bladder. Most tetrapods retained only the lungs, but during fetal development they show evidence that they once had gills.

A WALKING RELIC

Jeremy Dasen of the New York University Neuroscience Institute used genetics to help unravel secrets of movement in the first land animals. He studied little skates, a group of cartilaginous fish living on the bottom of the Atlantic Ocean off the East Coast of the United States. Little skates swim using large, sail-like fins. They also "walk" using smaller anterior pelvic fins. This walking movement shows the left-right alternating pattern used by all tetrapods. Dasen found that little skates have the same pattern of genes used in tetrapods that are required for left-right alternation. These genes were passed down from a common ancestor that lived 420 MYA, before vertebrates transitioned to land life.

FROM WATER TO LAND

The movement of vertebrates from water to land was a major evolutionary advance. It required changes in structure and function—respiration with lungs rather than gills, transformation of paired fins into limbs, and many changes in reproduction and development. Today, there are more than 28,000 species of tetrapods.[3]

Fish first moved from water to land more than 350 MYA, but this process did not happen just once. According to a study by Terry Ord and Georgina Cooke of Australia's University of New South Wales, it has happened at least 30 times. The pair collected examples of 130 species of still-living fish that spend time on land, including the American eel, the long-spined bullhead, and the Atlantic mudskipper. The authors found that 33 modern fish families have representatives that spend much of their time on land.[4] One

Diadectes was a large amphibian that was one of the first tetrapods that ate plants.

large coastal family, the blennies, has transitioned to land at least three times and perhaps up to seven. These amphibious fish seem to develop most often in intertidal zones, where their habitats are covered during high tide and exposed at low tide.

Two now-extinct fish groups, the osteolepiforms and the genus *Panderichthys*, were key in the transition from fish to amphibians, the first tetrapods. These two groups have more characteristics in common with primitive amphibians than with other fish. The common ancestor of *Panderichthys* and related species had a flattened skull and body, long snout, and no front dorsal fin. But there was a gap in fossils between *Panderichthys* and tetrapod fossils. The gap was filled in 2006 when a team led by Professor Neil Shubin of the University

Fred Mullison, fossil expert at the Academy of Natural Sciences of Drexel University, holds a cast of a *Tiktaalik roseae* fossil found in Arctic Canada.

of Chicago discovered a new fossil on Ellesmere Island in northern Canada. This fossil, named *Tiktaalik roseae* and referred to as a "fishapod," is midway between finned fish and amphibians with limbs. It was an important discovery. The fossil shows additional tetrapod-like traits, including a shortened skull top, a mobile neck, and wrist joints. *Tiktaalik* likely lived in shallow-water habitats.

In considering the transition to land, most paleontologists consider obvious tetrapod traits, such as lungs and limbs. But a 2017 study by neuroscientist Malcolm MacIver, paleontologist Lars Schmitz, and their colleagues looked at another factor—eyesight. The scientists found that better eyesight began developing millions of years before fish evolved functional limbs. In 59 groups of extinct fish, eye size tripled over a 12-million-year period.[5] In some groups, eyes migrated toward the top of the head, enabling the fish to see out of water. These changes in eye size and location greatly improved eyesight on land, making it much easier to hunt crawling organisms on the shoreline.

Lungfish and coelacanths had their heyday in the Devonian period. But the rise of other bony fish gradually took their place.

FISH WITH FINGERS

Like many paleontologists, Jenny Clack wondered how the first lobe-finned fish evolved limbs allowing them to live on land. In Greenland in 1987, she found a clue—the fossil of an early tetrapod, *Acanthostega*. This fishlike animal had both gills and lungs, but it probably spent most of its time in water. Its spine was weak, and its floppy legs would not support land locomotion. Its long tail was probably used for propulsion while swimming. But it had one key land feature: paddle-shaped fins that ended in tiny fingers. This suggests that fish likely evolved fingers before leaving the water.

Fish Bones

Not all fish have skeletons comprised of bone. Some, like the shark, have skeletons primarily consisting of cartilage. Bone provides strong muscle attachments. It also stores minerals. Vertebrates have two types of bone. Dermal bone is composed of plates and scales that develop in the skin. Examples are the bony armor of ostracoderms, shark scales, and the roof of the skull. Endoskeletal bone first forms as cartilage; it later forms bone as it collects calcium. Vertebrae, ribs, jaws, and limbs are endoskeletal bone.

Cartilaginous fish such as sharks have a skull to protect the brain and an attached jaw for biting, chewing, and tearing food. They also have a vertebral column that supports the fish and attaches the swimming muscles.

The head and jaw of today's ray-finned fish are much more complex than those of sharks and early ray-finned fish. The head and jaw include many new, small, highly interconnected bones.

Changes in vertebrae during bony fish evolution can be seen in modern fish. The ancient sturgeon has non-ossified vertebrae; that is, its vertebrae are cartilaginous rather than bony. This is an evolutionary reversal; the group once had a bony skeleton and returned to being cartilaginous. Its notochord is broken into sections similar to vertebrae.

Not all modern fish have bony skeletons similar to this one. Some, like sharks and rays, have cartilaginous skeletons.

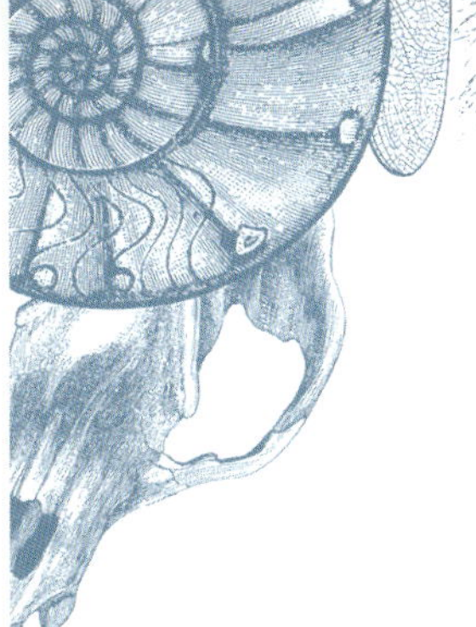

CHAPTER FIVE

The First Bony Fish

Class Osteichthyes, or bony fish, has two groups. Subclass Sarcopterygii includes lobe-finned fish and tetrapods. Sarcopterygians have fleshy fins attached to the body by a single bone. The larger subclass Actinopterygii includes ray-finned fish. Actinopterygians vary in the arrangement of their fins. Actinopterygian fins are composed of webs of skin attached to the body by a fan-shaped arrangement of bony spines. They are supported at the base by parallel rows of bones. The spines are analogous to fingers, but the fish lack the arm bones present in tetrapods. This subclass contains about 33,433 species, or more than

The bony spines on a walleye's dorsal fin support webbed skin that attaches to the fish's body.

one-half of all vertebrate species.[1] They are found in all aquatic habitats and are a major food source for millions of people.

CHARACTERISTICS OF BONY AND RAY-FINNED FISH

Bony fish can be identified by a number of common characteristics. All have skeletons made of true bone, although the bone has been secondarily lost in a few species. That is, at one point in their evolution, these fish had bone, but as evolution continued, they lost it. They have a bony structure called an operculum covering the gill arches. They have lungs or swim bladders, though some bottom-dwelling species have lost them.

As a clade of bony fish, the ray-finned fish have all of these characteristics plus several distinguishing features of their own. Like sharks, most ray-finned fish have a rounded body shape that is tapered at both ends, making swimming

RAY-FINNED FISH STRUCTURE

The largemouth bass is a typical ray-finned fish. It has paired eyes and nostrils and a bony operculum protecting the gill openings. The paired pectoral and pelvic fins help the fish steer and stop, an anal fin and one or two dorsal fins keep it upright, and a caudal (tail) fin propels it forward. Fins may have spiny or soft rays. The lateral line senses underwater vibrations. The vent is the opening for the digestive, urinary, and reproductive tracts. Some ray-finned fish lack certain of these characteristics; ocean sunfish, for example, lack a tail fin. However, these features are typical of most ray-finned fish.

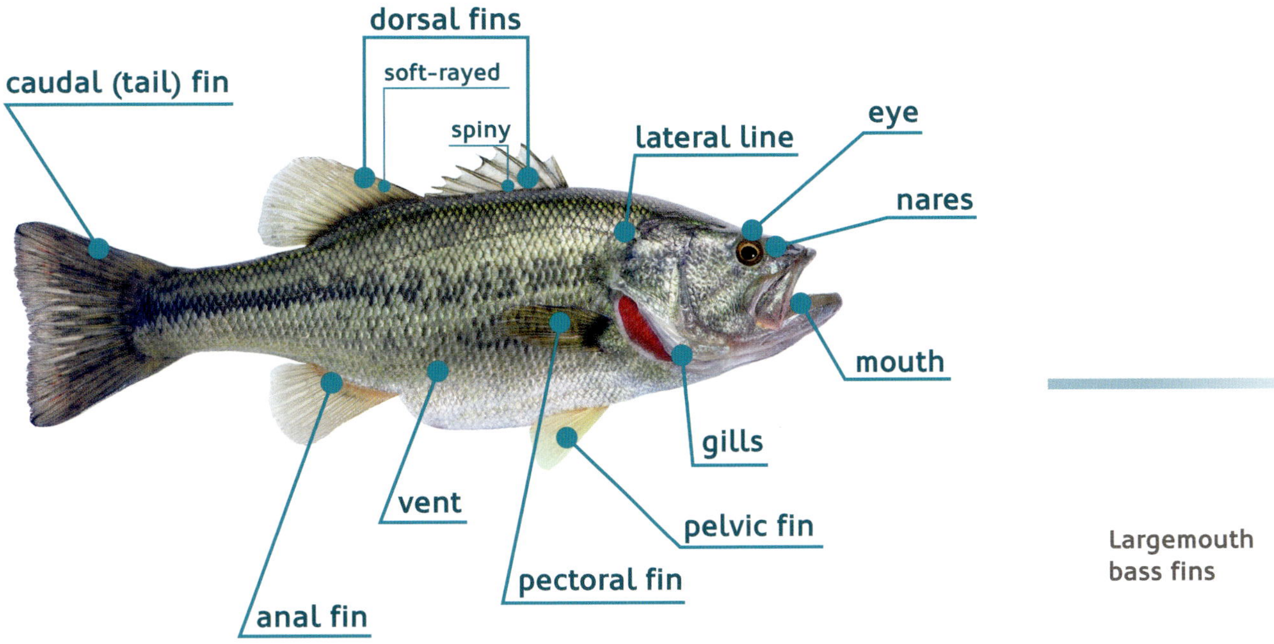

Largemouth bass fins

easier. They have fin rays that attach fins to the body. They also have long, curved bones under the operculum that support the gills and may aid in breathing.

THE EARLIEST BONY FISH

The Devonian period, from 416 to 359 MYA, is known as the Age of Fishes. It was a time of major geologic and climatic changes on Earth. The southern supercontinent Gondwana was moving northward from the South Pole toward the equator. A second supercontinent, Laurasia, formed in the Northern Hemisphere and straddled the equator. Meanwhile, in Earth's oceans

Gondwana and Laurasia were formed when the supercontinent Pangaea broke up. Gondwana drifted south, while Laurasia drifted north.

and freshwaters, a succession of fish groups dominated. Jawless fish were gradually replaced by armored placoderms, which in turn gave way to cartilaginous fish and finally to bony fish, including both lobe-fins and ray-fins. Placoderms went extinct, but representatives of all other fish groups of that time remain. Cartilaginous and bony fish were both dominant. The Devonian period ended with a massive extinction that killed 70 percent of marine life.[2] No one is sure of the cause.

During this busy Devonian period, about 420 MYA, two species of fish, *Andreolepis hedei* and *Lophosteus superbus*, lived in the area that is now the Baltic Sea. These sardine-sized fish showed a characteristic not seen in previous fish—their teeth grew from their jawbones rather than from their gums, as shark teeth do. According to Philippe Janvier of the National Museum of Natural History in Paris, these fossils are transitional fossils, with characteristics of both sharks and bony fish. Janvier says the fossils represent a "very modest" beginning for the modern arrangement of teeth implanted in jaws.[3] Twenty million years later, the first

GIANT "DINO-FISH"

During the Triassic, Jurassic, and Cretaceous periods, between 252 and 65 MYA, dinosaurs were not the only giants on Earth. A few species of fish were large enough to earn the nickname "dino-fish." *Leedsichthys*, from the Jurassic period, was 70 feet (21 m) long.[4] By comparison, the blue whale ranges from 82 to 105 feet (25 to 32 m).[5] Like the blue whale, *Leedsichthys* ate plankton and krill. *Xiphactinus*, the largest known bony fish during the late Cretaceous, was a mere 20 feet (6 m) long, but it was a ferocious predator.[6] One specimen contains the nearly intact remains of a 10-foot (3 m) long fish called *Gillicus*.[7] Paleontologists assume this *Xiphactinus* died soon after swallowing its prey. Giant sharks also roamed these ancient seas. At least two fossil sharks from this time period, *Squalicorax* and *Cretoxyrhina*, contained *Xiphactinus* remains. *Cretoxyrhina* was 25 feet (8 m) long.[8] Other sharks of this time period ranged from 30 feet (9 m) long to the largest known shark, *Megalodon*, which reached 45 to 60 feet (14 to 18 m) in length.[9] Many *Xiphactinus* and other marine fossils have been found in Kansas, which was covered by a shallow sea during the Cretaceous period.

AN ABUNDANCE OF *KNIGHTIA*

Knightia is the opposite of a rare fossil. This six-inch (15 cm) fish was extremely common during the Eocene period, 55–35 MYA. So many fossils of *Knightia* were found in the Green River formation in Wyoming that it is now the Wyoming state fossil. This small fish looked and acted like herring and was originally classified in the herring genus *Clupea*. Like herring, *Knightia* formed huge schools throughout North American lakes and rivers. It fed on small floating plankton and was food for large predators—in this case, *Diplomystus* and *Mioplosus*. *Knightia*'s abundance highlights its great importance in Eocene food webs.

modern-looking bony fish appeared. They had much larger teeth, large enough for bony fish to become predators.

By the end of the Devonian period, ray-finned fish were dominant. Until the Jurassic period, about 201 MYA, most ray-finned fish belonged to a group called palaeoniscoids. These were small fish with scales covered by a shiny, mineralized material called ganoine. Palaeoniscoids were diverse, resembling many modern bony fish from eels to angelfish. They were extinct by the end of the Cretaceous period, about 65 MYA. Present-day relatives of palaeoniscoids include sturgeons, paddlefish, and bichirs. Little is known about the evolution of these groups because fossil records are very sparse.

By about 340 MYA, ray-fins were the dominant fish in the oceans. But modern fish evolved into their present diversity much later, beginning about 66 MYA.

HEMOGLOBIN, CAPILLARIES, AND SWIM BLADDERS

Michael Berenbrink and colleagues at the University of Liverpool showed that specialized hemoglobin developed only once during fish evolution. About 250 MYA, a capillary network around fishes' eyes developed. Fish with this structure survived better. The specialized hemoglobin increased oxygen levels, and the capillary network delivered more oxygen to the eyes, improving eyesight. Later fish retained this structure. About 150 MYA, a second capillary network developed for the swim bladder. This network arose four times in different fish groups.

SWIM BLADDERS

Most fish have a single swim bladder, but in some (for example, the bichir *Polypterus*), the organ is paired. In bichirs, lungfish, and others, the inner surface of the swim bladder has many blood vessels and tiny air sacs. Thus, the swim bladder has a role in breathing as well as floating. This function seems to suggest that lungs developed from swim bladders; however, lungs appeared first in evolution. The exact origin of swim bladders cannot be determined for certain, due to a lack of fossil evidence. One hypothesis is that the swim bladder evolved from early paired lung pouches, which

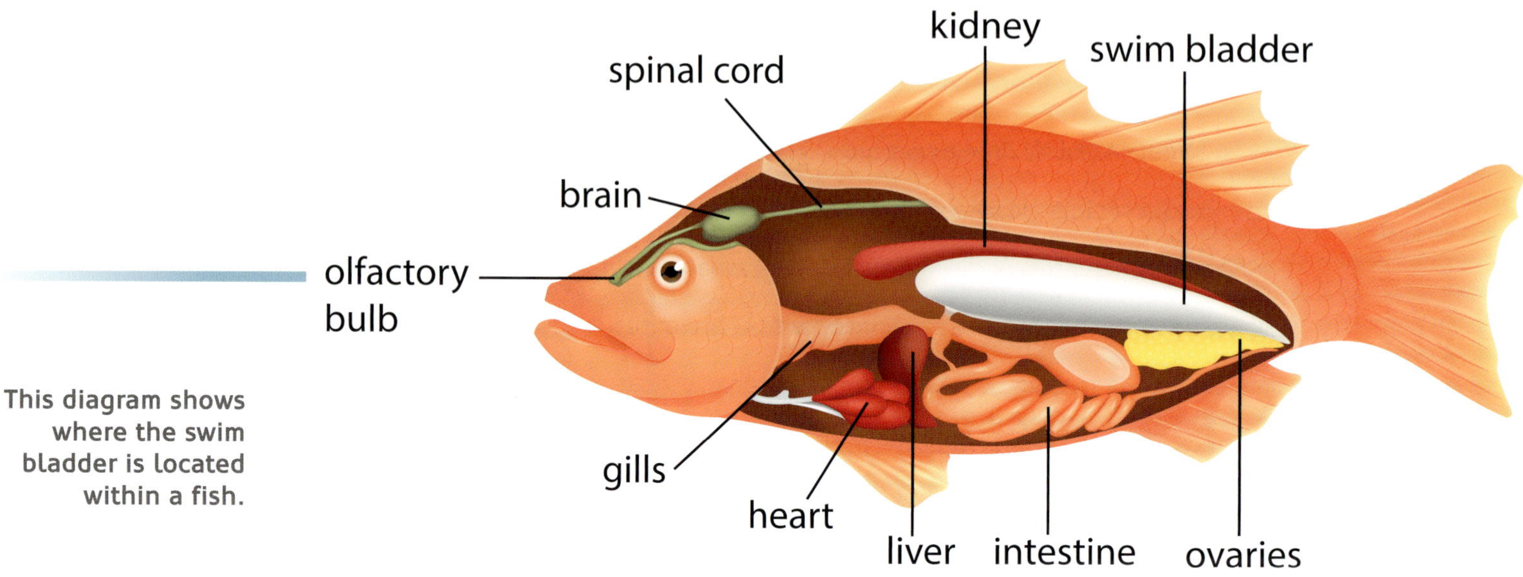

This diagram shows where the swim bladder is located within a fish.

gradually fused. According to a 2016 study by scientists at Jikei University in Tokyo, Japan, swim bladders originally developed from simple lungs.

Some swim bladders are directly connected to the fish's intestinal tract. The fish gulps air at the surface to inflate the bladder and releases air through the mouth or vent to deflate it. Other swim bladders are self-contained, not connected to the intestinal tract. They do not depend on gulping or releasing air at the surface but are filled and emptied using gases carried in the bloodstream. Blood passing through the swim bladder wall becomes acidic due to the release of carbon dioxide and lactic acid. This acidity decreases the ability of oxygen to bind to hemoglobin. Hemoglobin is a part of blood that transports oxygen through the body. To better bind the oxygen, fish have a different form of hemoglobin than other animals. A thick network of tiny blood vessels in the swim bladder, running in opposite directions, also concentrates the oxygen and enables it to transfer from hemoglobin back into the swim bladder. In 2005, physiologists Michael Berenbrink and colleagues at the University of Liverpool, England, studied living fish species representing different stages of fish evolution. They showed that specialized hemoglobin evolved first, followed much later by the evolution of the network of blood vessels.

Much of the fish radiation, particularly in teleosts (by far the largest group within the ray-finned fish), has occurred in the most recent geologic era. But many key structures necessary for successful aquatic life evolved earlier, in the Devonian period. These adaptations still appear, in one form or another, in all living fish.

Ornate bichirs have lungs, enabling them to breathe air in standing-water habitats.

CHAPTER SIX

Modern Orders of Bony Fish

Modern bony fish, in the class Osteichthyes, are the largest and most diverse group of vertebrates, making up 95 percent of all vertebrates. Of their two subclasses, Actinopterygii (ray-finned fish) are much more numerous than Sarcopterygii (lobe-finned fish).[1]

Living ray-finned species are separated into two groups that are very different in form. The smaller of these two actinopterygian groups is the family of bichirs. They are long, ancient-looking predators from African lakes. The remaining ray-finned fish include the 27 species of holosteans (sturgeons and paddlefish) and the neopterygians (gars, bowfin, and teleosts). There is a single living family of gars and a single species of bowfin. Almost all living fish species—33,384 of the 33,433 species of ray-finned fish—are teleosts.[2]

BICHIRS

Bichirs, native to Africa, are the most ancient living bony fish. Scientists are studying bichirs for clues to the evolution of tetrapods. According to Carl Zimmer, writing for *National Geographic*, they are looking for "some of the mutations that reprogrammed fins into feet."[3] A bichir "walks" over the river or lake bottom. It uses its pelvic fins to raise its head and torso and then pushes forward with its back end.

Scientists at McGill University in Montreal decided to see how bichirs would fare on land. They raised baby bichirs for eight months in a pebble-lined terrarium, misted to keep the fishes' skin moist. These bichirs learned to walk

RECLASSIFYING BICHIRS

For years, bichirs were classified with coelacanths and lungfish because of their lungs, lobed fins, and bottom-dwelling habit. But they are now considered actinopterygians because their fins have rays. The group consists of two genera: a single species of *Erpetoichthys*, commonly known as ropefish or reedfish, and at least 11 species of bichirs, genus *Polypterus*. Bichirs' many dorsal fins give them a dragon-like appearance, and their extremely hard scales have been studied as a model for human body armor.

much more efficiently than their African river counterparts, using shorter steps, smaller tail movements, and less fin flapping. In short, they were more graceful. Their bodies also changed. Shoulder bones became less connected, allowing greater arm/fin movement. These bones also became bigger and stronger, providing better lift. Changes seen in these bichirs mirror changes paleontologists have seen in the fish ancestors of tetrapods. According to Zimmer, "It's as if the bichirs are replaying evolution in their own lifetime."[4]

HOLOSTEANS: STURGEONS AND PADDLEFISH

Twenty-seven species of living sturgeons and shovelnoses and two species of paddlefish reside in the Northern Hemisphere.[5] Most live in freshwater rivers and lakes, but some live in shallow seas and enter rivers to spawn. One of the paddlefish species, the Chinese paddlefish, may now be extinct. None have been caught by fishers in the Yangtze River since 2003, and no young have been seen since 1995.

Sturgeons include some of the world's largest freshwater fish, with maximum sizes reaching 28.2 feet (8.6 m).[6] Most of the skeleton is cartilaginous, with bones only in the skull, jaws, and pectoral girdle. The vertebral column extends into the asymmetric tail fin, as in sharks. This characteristic has been retained from ancestors. Their bodies have five rows of bony shields, but

they lack the lateral lines and scales their ancestors had. They have an elongated snout with four sensory barbels, or fleshy filaments. Paddlefish have similar features but have two instead of four barbels. They have a giant rostrum—a long, beak-like projection—on the head. Paddlefish have only tiny patches of scales and no shields.

Early sturgeons date back to about 200 MYA, when they coexisted with dinosaurs. According to dinosaur paleontologist Jack Horner, "When sturgeons were swimming through the waters, there were *Tyrannosaurus rex* walking in Montana."[7] Sturgeons have

ENDANGERED STURGEONS

Sturgeons have survived longer than most living species, but they may now be in danger of extinction. All 29 species of sturgeons and paddlefish are on the International Union for Conservation of Nature (IUCN) list of endangered species, making them the world's most threatened group of species.[8] Seventeen species are classified as Highly Endangered, the highest threat level. Some are endangered due to overfishing. People collect caviar, the females' unfertilized eggs, as a delicacy. Other species could no longer reach their spawning grounds when rivers were dammed. At least four species may already be extinct.[9]

Unfertilized eggs are removed from a female sturgeon and sold as caviar.

survived major extinctions, ice ages, changes in river courses, and other geologic and climatic changes.

Sturgeons look prehistoric, as though they have not changed for millions of years, but in some ways, they are evolving rapidly. A University of Michigan study points out that sturgeons have evolved a huge range of body sizes, from bass-sized dwarfs to car-sized giants. The study analyzed rates of evolution in nearly 8,000 fish species. It tested the hypothesis that rates of species formation correlate with anatomical change—that is, diverse species groups show greater variations in anatomy, while groups with fewer species vary less. In general, this hypothesis held true. Gars, with few species, show little range in body size and form species very slowly. The salmon family (containing salmon, trout, whitefish, and char), with many species, show a great range of body sizes and form species rapidly. But sturgeon do not fit this pattern—they are a small group with great variation in body size.

In the Great Lakes, the environment is changing rapidly. It is degrading due to pollution and habitat loss. Climate change is increasing temperatures. The environmental cues on which sturgeons depend for determining the right time to spawn or hatch are changing. Studies on lake sturgeon support the idea of rapid evolution. The environment affects sturgeons' egg incubation time, egg size, and larval size. Incubation time decreases as the temperature increases. Early-spawning females lay larger eggs, and the resulting larvae are larger than those of later-spawning females.

NEOPTERYGIANS: GARS AND BOWFINS

The neopterygians branched off later in evolution than bichirs and sturgeons. Two neopterygian groups, gars and bowfins, are small and retain some characteristics of earlier fish. Gars form

The garfish has a slender body and long rows of sharp teeth. It is able to survive for hours outside of water.

a single family of seven species. Bowfins are now represented by a single living species, *Amia calva*.

Like sturgeons, gars look almost prehistoric and appear to have changed little in the past 100 million years. They are hungry predators with long tubular bodies, large elongated

Bowfins live in eastern North America, where they prefer backwaters with a slow current.

snouts, and mouths full of sharp teeth. They have hard, interlocking scales and a specialized swim bladder that doubles as a lung, so they can breathe air when necessary. Gars can get very large—up to ten feet (3 m) long and 300 pounds (136 kg) in weight.[10] They are primarily freshwater fish. They once appeared on several continents, but now they live only in North and Central America.

Adult bowfins range from 1.6 to 3.3 feet (0.5–1 m) long and weigh 1 to 5 pounds (0.5–2.3 kg).[11] The bowfin's dorsal fin extends along most of its body length and has more than 45 rays. The vertebral column extends into the top part of the rounded tail fin. The head lacks scales. Bowfins, too, can breathe both air and water, giving them an advantage in low-oxygen situations.

Such "living fossils" are important in research, helping scientists understand evolutionary changes and better analyze disease in vertebrates, including humans. The spotted gar, for example, has a genome, or complete set of genes, that is highly conserved. This means that it retains many genes and even whole chromosomes exactly as they were in bony vertebrate ancestors. Conserved genes are usually genes essential to the organism's survival. In the gar's case, they control functions such as immunity, development, and bone mineralization. Studying the gar helps scientists compare evolution before and after teleosts.

The seahorse is a uniquely shaped teleost.

CHAPTER SEVEN

Early Teleost Groups

The teleost clade is vast and diverse. Its 33,000-plus species vary in size and shape from eels to herrings to tunas to seahorses.[1] They live in ponds, lakes, rivers, and oceans, and even in caves and on the seafloor. Because the group is so large and complex, scientists have had difficulty unraveling its relationships and developing a meaningful phylogeny, or description of relationships. Most studies have been based either on fossils or on the structure and development of living fish. But a 2013 study developed a fish "tree of life" based on comparison of DNA sequences in 1,410 bony fish species, two chondrichthyans, and four tetrapod groups.[2] According to the study's authors, the evolutionary tree

The anglerfish is a teleost that has evolved strong jaws that extend outward, allowing it to swallow prey twice its size.

generally agrees with past trees based on morphological characteristics, but it clarifies the existence of more clades.

Three major anatomical features—scales, tails, and jaws—underwent tremendous changes when teleosts evolved from their ancestors. Early actinopterygians, such as gars and sturgeons, had ganoid scales, which are thick and tough. Ganoid scales contain the substance ganoine, derived from the same enamel found in human teeth. Teleost scales are either cycloid or ctenoid; both types are thin, flexible, and rounded like an egg. Ctenoid scales have sharp barbs around their back edges. Losing ganoine increased the flexibility and decreased the weight of teleost scales. This improved the fishes' swimming ability, making them more efficient predators or more elusive prey.

Teleosts evolved a symmetrical tail in which the two lobes are equal in size and the spinal cord does not extend into the upper lobe. Teleost jaws became progressively stronger. Early ray-finned fish had snapping jaws with weak closing muscles. In neopterygians, jaws close more strongly. Also, the upper jaw moved forward and to the sides, making the mouth larger and creating suction to draw prey into the mouth. Suction increased further as the fish evolved a tube-like, protruding mouth.

WHOLE GENOME DUPLICATION

Sometimes, during the making of eggs and sperm or the dividing of cells in the early embryo, a gene duplication may occur. A single

DNA MARKERS AND FISH RELATIONSHIPS

New, more precise studies of evolutionary relationships are now possible because of the use of DNA markers. Both parents contribute nuclear DNA, which is present in the nuclei of all cells. Mitochondria, the energy-processing parts of cells, also contain DNA: mitochondrial DNA, or mtDNA. Organisms inherit mtDNA only from their mothers. Pieces of either nuclear or mtDNA can be sequenced and used as markers. DNA markers are sequences of DNA that provide a common measurement of evolutionary data across a wide variety of species. The 2013 "tree of life" study of fish evolution used 20 nuclear markers and one mitochondrial DNA marker. Scientists compared these markers in all 1,416 species of fish to determine how many markers matched in the various species.[3] Making these detailed comparisons across all fish species enabled scientists to develop a complex tree showing relationships among the examined species. It could be used as a framework for placing all fish studied.

TELEOST SCALES

Teleosts have rounded cycloid or ctenoid scales that overlap, increasing their flexibility. Cycloid scales have smooth edges; ctenoid scales have a spiny back edge. Both types have two layers: a bony surface layer containing calcium salts and a deeper layer containing collagen, a type of protein. The scales grow as the fish grows, producing growth rings that can be used to determine the fish's age. Cycloid and ctenoid scales are modified from the ganoid scales found in actinopterygians such as bichirs, gars, and sturgeons.

gene, a whole chromosome, or even a whole genome may be duplicated. It is now well established that a whole genome duplication (WGD) happened in teleosts. This has affected the clade's entire evolution. This event is referred to as teleost-specific WGD, or TS-WGD. The duplicated genes in a WGD have different fates. Many lose their functions; others may evolve new functions. Either way, WGD provides huge amounts of new material for evolution. It leads to diversification and speeds up evolution.

Researchers have found strong evidence for duplication of several groups of genes in teleosts. The genes shown to be duplicated are general-purpose genes that are found in most organisms. For example, they include the genes that direct how body parts are organized during development. There are two sets of these in teleosts, but only one set in other organisms. Scientists think groups that have undergone WGD are more robust and less prone to extinction than other groups. They may adapt more rapidly to changing environments. Genes that regulate major body functions are particularly likely to lead to evolutionary breakthroughs. WGD very likely contributed to the rapid evolution of teleosts into thousands of new species.

ELECTRIC FISH

After the TS-WGD, groups began to split off. They were still teleosts, but they diversified in unique ways. One adaptation was the ability to generate electricity. Darwin identified six fish

THE BIOLOGICAL BASIS OF WGD

Body cells in organisms contain paired chromosomes. One member of each pair comes from the mother, and one comes from the father. During evolution, the whole genome sometimes duplicates. This results in each cell having two pairs of each chromosome instead of one. This can happen in one of two ways. First, when eggs and sperm are made, the chromosomes are normally halved; that is, only one member of a pair goes into each egg or sperm cell. When duplication occurs, this halving of chromosomes does not occur. Second, the chromosomes may double after fertilization, when the embryo's cells are dividing. During evolution, some of these new copies of chromosomes may be lost. Others may take on new functions. Whatever happens, whole genome duplication speeds up evolution and increases diversity in that group.

Electric eels deliver a more powerful shock when they leap from the water than when they stay underwater.

lineages with electric organs and concluded that all evolved independently. A 2014 University of Wisconsin study analyzed DNA from the cells of fishes' electric organs. Of 25,000 genes, they identified about 100 that appeared to be involved in electrical activity.[4] According to study coauthor Jason Gallant, cells of the electric organs, called electrocytes, were once muscle cells. Genes that control the ability to contract in these cells are turned off, and genes that control electrical generation are turned on.

Each cell in the electric eel produces approximately 50 millivolts of electricity. When charges from all cells accumulate, the fish can generate up to 600 volts. Michael Sussman, coauthor of the Wisconsin study, says, "There's enough power in the eel's electric organ to kill anything it wants."[5] But using electricity for hunting is rare. Most fish use it for navigation in murky river habitats much like a bat uses echolocation. Any object in the water disrupts the eel's electric field, enabling it to pinpoint that object. Fish also use electricity for communication. African elephant fish species recognize each other by individuals' unique frequencies or patterns. As Darwin deduced, many fish have independently evolved electrical abilities. Some of the six lineages he identified contain hundreds of species.

AN EXPLOSION OF TELEOST RADIATION

Electricity is only one example of adaptation in teleosts. Catfish have spread throughout the world, inhabiting rivers and streams everywhere except polar regions. They account for 11 percent of all fish species.[6] The synodontids, native to Africa, are known as "squeaker catfish" because of their high-pitched vocalizations. They also exhibit unusual breeding behaviors. *Synodontis multipunctatus* is a brood parasite. In Lake Tanganyika, this catfish mixes its eggs with the eggs of other fish species. The baby catfish grow faster than their hosts and feed on them.

In 2009, Jeremy Wright, a graduate student at the University of Michigan, determined that at least 1,250 and possibly more than 1,600 species of catfish are venomous.[7] They have venom glands near bony spines on their dorsal and pectoral fins. The spines lock into place when a fish is threatened, and the venom is released when it jabs the spine into a predator. North American fishers have suffered painful stings; in some parts of the world, stings may be fatal. Of all fish species, 2,386–2,962 species have been found to be venomous.[8]

Since their appearance on Earth, humans have become a major selective pressure, acting on other species—including teleosts—and affecting their evolution, not always in a positive way. Humans are affecting pink salmon by overfishing. Since the 1960s, the average size of pink salmon has decreased by 30 percent.[9] This decrease is not caused by fishers catching the oldest and largest fish, since returning salmon are all the same age. They go downstream to the ocean immediately after hatching and return

WALL-CLIMBING CATFISH

In 2015, Geoff Hoese, a naturalist and cave explorer, led a team of scientists through a limestone cave in Ecuador. The explorers observed small cave catfish climb a wall to a height of ten feet (3 m) before dropping back into the water. These fish—suckermouth armored catfish—attach to rocks with their mouths to prevent washing downstream. The mouths, skin, and fins of cave catfish have different adaptations than river catfish. Hoese suggests these catfish may represent a small evolutionary step as this species colonizes a new niche.

exactly two years later to the same stream, where they spawn and die. Instead, the size decrease shows evolution at work. Salmon now have slower growth rates and are smaller at maturity. With no fishing pressure, salmon would grow larger and produce more eggs. Because fishers select larger salmon, the smaller salmon are more likely to survive and return to their streams to spawn.

Finally, there is evidence that salmon can evolve very quickly—even in a single generation. Again, humans are the selective pressure, according to a 19-year study at Oregon State University on hatchery-raised steelhead salmon. The hatchery fish show rapid genetic changes that help them live under hatchery conditions. However, once in the wild, hatchery salmon are less able to produce offspring that can survive in wild rivers. According to Mark Christie, lead author on the Oregon State University study, "To see these changes happen in a single generation was amazing. Evolutionary change doesn't always take thousands of years."[10]

Recently, humans have been one major selective pressure driving evolution. But over millennia, many forces have interacted to produce diversity. These forces have included everything from predators to climate change to natural disasters.

CHAPTER EIGHT

The Percomorph Clade

As teleosts progressed through evolution, their species numbers exploded and they radiated throughout many habitats and ecological niches. Of all the orders and suborders of teleosts, by far the largest is the Percomorpha clade. In the 2016 book *Fishes of the World*, J. S. Nelson and colleagues described a reclassification of percomorphs based on newly collected DNA evidence. The new clade consists of 13 orders, several of which were previously grouped into the order Perciformes. This older order included more than 10,000 species and was considered polyphyletic, meaning its species had more than one ancestor.[1]

When threatened, the puffer fish puffs up to twice its normal size by gulping water.

Percomorphs are the world's most diverse group of fish. They include more than one-third of all ray-finned fish, with an immense variety of sizes, body types, and niches. Among the many types of fish included in this group are gobies, cichlids, flying fish, topminnows, jacks, bettas, flatfish, seahorses, tunas, wrasses, perches, scorpion fish, guppies, and puffers.

PERCOMORPHS AND POLYTOMIES

Percomorphs are certainly not the only group of teleosts, but they are uniquely suited for illustrating adaptive radiation, the process by which their incredible diversity formed. During adaptive radiation, vast numbers of new species develop very rapidly, in terms of evolutionary time. This process often occurs after a major environmental change. For example, an extinction event may open many new ecological niches. Percomorphs underwent adaptive radiation after the Cretaceous-Paleogene (K-Pg) mass extinction approximately 66 MYA.

Percomorphs have the typical teleost body plan, including fin placement, scales, and jaws. At the same time, they have evolved so many variations in form that determining evolutionary relationships by comparing body types is almost impossible. Scientists have addressed this difficulty in cladograms by placing groups with the same ancestor but unknown relationships together as part of a polytomy—a node having more than two distinct lineages.

An artist's drawing shows land and sea creatures during the Cretaceous period, prior to a mass extinction event.

The position of the lineages in the cladogram says nothing about their relationships to other groups in the polytomy. It only indicates that they have the same ancestor. Only recently have scientists begun to unravel these relationships by comparing DNA sequences in fish groups traditionally placed in polytomies. These studies show that the major radiation of percomorphs into new subgroups occurred in the first ten million years of the Cenozoic era, just after the K-Pg mass extinction.

ADAPTIVE RADIATION AND CICHLID SUPERFLOCKS

Rapid radiation within a relatively defined area, such as a lake or island, can result in the formation of what are known as superflocks. These are groups of distinct but closely related species. In the past 150,000 years, there has been an explosion of cichlids in the Lake Victoria region of East Africa. These small, colorful, perch-like fish have radiated to form a superflock of more than 700 species. DNA studies are beginning to uncover how this happened. In 2014, Russell Fernald of Stanford University and his international colleagues sequenced the genomes of five cichlids from this region—the Nile tilapia, which was the ancestral lineage, and four cichlid species

REVERSE EVOLUTION

Fishers usually practice size-selective fishing by taking the largest fish. Over time, the species begins to mature earlier, and the fish caught are smaller. By the 1970s, Lake Michigan's yellow perch fishery was overfished. Perch in this area were maturing at two years of age, rather than the normal three to four years. When the commercial fishery closed in 1996, scientists thought it would take hundreds, perhaps thousands, of years for the perch to return to their original size and reproductive age. But once the selective pressure of fishing was removed, this so-called reverse evolution happened in only two decades.

Lake Victoria is Africa's largest lake. It borders Tanzania, Uganda, and Kenya.

that evolved at distinct times in separate lake or river locations. DNA analyses showed gene duplication rates six times higher than normal in all species. They also identified 40 previously unknown regulatory genes.[2] The presence of these new genes indicates rapid evolution.

Catherine Wagner of the University of Wyoming led another international project describing how this rapid evolution occurred. The team analyzed more than 3 million DNA sites in the genome of 100 cichlid species and published its results in 2017. Wagner's team found that the ancestor of Lake Victoria's explosion of diversity was a hybrid of two cichlid species originating from different drainage basins, the Upper Nile and the Congo rivers. The species likely hybridized about 150,000 years ago when the wet climate allowed the Congo lineage to colonize lakes in the region and to encounter the Upper Nile species. The new hybrid species began to radiate within the lakes. Following a dry climatic period, Lake Victoria filled up again about 15,000 years ago, and descendants of the hybrids recolonized the lake. These

CAN LAKE VICTORIA CICHLIDS SURVIVE HUMANS?

Human activity is devastating cichlid populations in Africa's Lake Victoria. In the 1960s, the Nile perch was introduced into the lake to generate a fishing industry and feed the local people. But Nile perch are large—up to 6.6 feet (2 m) long—and they eat cichlids.[4] Perch numbers exploded. By the mid-1980s, approximately two-thirds of Lake Victoria's cichlid diversity was gone.

Nutrient pollution is driving another stage of cichlid evolution. Nutrient pollution lowers oxygen levels and makes the water murky. Remaining female cichlids are less able to see potential mates, which they choose by their bright colors. Species are hybridizing, and once bright red and blue males are being replaced by dull brown fish. At the same time, cichlids are losing their specialized feeding habits. A few hybrids now seem to be exploiting previously unused habitats, suggesting that new hybridized gene combinations might eventually help restore diversity. But if cichlid diversity recovers, it will be through a new group of species adapted to different conditions.

descendants have since radiated to form at least 500 new cichlid species colonizing many ecological niches. The cichlid radiation is particularly astonishing in view of the fact that more than 40 other fish species that colonized Lake Victoria at the same time have barely changed. Wagner describes the cichlid radiation as "one of the most spectacular examples of the evolution of modern biodiversity."[3]

EXAMPLES OF PERCOMORPH VARIATION

One of the strangest cases of adaptation among percomorphs are the flatfish, including food fish such as soles, halibuts, and plaices. The adults in this fish group have both eyes on the same side of the head. In each individual's early life, the

The flounder is a flatfish that has both eyes on one side of the body.

eye migrates from one side to the opposite side of the skull. Flatfish live on the ocean floor. They rest on the eyeless side, with both eyes facing upward, able to view predators or prey. Flatfish eggs rise from the bottom to the ocean surface, where they hatch into completely symmetrical fish. After a few weeks, the tiny larvae metamorphose into the adult form and then sink to the bottom. This bizarre adaptation is obviously beneficial—currently more than 800 species of flatfish have been described.

Scientists have disagreed about whether all flatfish arose from a single ancestor. A 2016 study from the University of Oxford in England, led by Matt Friedman, shed new light on the

TUNAS AND SHARKS CONVERGE

Thanks to convergent evolution, sharks and tunas have evolved a similar body form for underwater swimming. Both have a rigid front end and a highly flexible tail end with a crescent-shaped tail fin. By moving the tail end in a wavelike motion and barely moving the front end, they can swim rapidly while keeping their eyes focused on the prey ahead. They can also accelerate in short bursts and snatch prey quickly. Finally, both groups can keep their body temperature high in cold water. These features evolved separately, after sharks and tunas diverged from their common ancestor more than 400 MYA. This suggests that the open ocean environment selects for this type of locomotion.

subject. The group used DNA sequencing to study ultraconserved DNA elements (UCEs). These UCEs are DNA sequences that remain the same even in distantly related species, for example, fish and humans. Comparing UCEs can be extremely useful for settling questions about evolutionary relationships. Friedman's study looked at more than 1,000 regions of the genome in 45 flatfish species. The results indicated that flatfish evolved only once, from a single ancestor.[5]

Finally, a much more ordinary percomorph, the guppy, has been used to illustrate how natural selection operates. In 1990, three scientists—David N. Reznick, Heather Bryga, and John A. Endler—tested a mathematical theory relating to reproductive behavior, which is central to natural selection. The theory proposed that animals preyed on as adults will have many offspring at a young age and die early. In contrast, animals preyed on while young will have fewer, larger offspring later in life.

The researchers moved a group of guppies from a river in Trinidad to a small tributary. The adult river guppies had been preyed upon by larger predatory cichlids. The guppies living in the tributary were eaten as young by small killifish, their only predator. Scientists watched the guppies for 11 years, or 30–60 generations.[6] During that time, the river guppies evolved. They began to mature later, grow larger, and have fewer young—just as the theory predicted. The result provides evidence to back up the mathematical prediction.

Percomorphs are the largest, most diverse fish group. Until recently, knowledge of their evolution has been sparse, but recent genetic studies are beginning to fill in the blanks. A new era in the study of fish evolution is just beginning.

Fish Evolution Today

Fish have been evolving on Earth for the last 518 million years, but only for the past few hundred of those years have humans been trying to understand the path of fish evolution. The process has not been easy. The rarity of fossils translates to many gaps in fish history. Evolutionary biologists now use the technique of gene sequencing to compare DNA among living fish. Changes in DNA sequences in various fish groups can show their relationships and provide a roadmap of the order in which groups likely appeared. Today, new fossils continue to be found, DNA studies are proceeding rapidly, and evolutionary biologists continue to ask new questions about the origin and evolution of fish on Earth.

Scientists study modern fish to help understand the evolutionary path fish have taken over millions of years.

QUESTIONS SCIENTISTS ASK

One of many questions scientists have asked is, "Why are teleosts the dominant fish type?" Teleosts arose approximately 260 MYA, about halfway through fish evolution, and today they make up 96 percent of all fish and more than one-half of all vertebrates. The prevailing view has been that teleosts out-competed other groups because they have always been more innovative. But a recent DNA study casts doubt on this assumption. Scientists John Clarke, Graeme T. Lloyd, and Matt Friedman analyzed 1,000 fossils from 500 species of holosteans—gars and bowfins—and teleosts from the first 160 million years of teleost evolution.[1] Holosteans were dominant before teleosts, and the study found that they, too, were highly diverse in size and shape. It appears that holosteans evolved at least as rapidly as teleosts, and possibly more rapidly. This finding suggests

FISH OUT OF WATER

Blennies in the South Pacific Ocean are trying to escape predators by relocating to land. They spend low tide in rock pools on the coast. At high tide, they climb onto the rocks, avoiding the flounders and lionfish that want to eat them. Scientists tested how dangerous the water was by submerging models of blennies in the ocean. The models they retrieved had bite marks and pieces missing. The risk of being eaten on land is only about one-third of that in water for blennies.[2] Several blenny species have already become land-dwellers. They still breathe with gills, but stronger tail fins help them jump between rocks.

The mudskipper is a fish that lives in Africa, Polynesia, and Australia. It has the ability to pull itself along on land with its fins.

that something other than superior innovation must account for teleosts' rapid evolution. The question of what this might be is still open.

Scientists also continue to be fascinated by the transition of fish into tetrapods. Research from New York University indicates that, to leave the water, ancient pre-tetrapods needed not only limbs but also a specialized brain structure. The brain needed to allow for the fins to move separately, alternating as in walking. Scientists find it unlikely that this brain structure evolved

DEPTH AND EVOLUTION

Most ocean species are restricted by depth, because the ocean environment changes drastically from top to bottom. The deep ocean is darker and colder, food is scarcer, and pressures are higher. But populations of the North Atlantic roundnose grenadier live at depths ranging from 590 to 8,500 feet (180 to 2,600 m).[3] The genomes of deep-water populations are specialized in ways not found in those in shallower depths. It appears that all genotypes of grenadiers mate by meeting in spawning groups, where they release eggs and sperm into the water to mix randomly. The larvae then float around at the same depth, approximately 3,900 feet (1,200 m), before moving to a depth based on their genome.[4] This spawning method deepens the mystery of how grenadiers maintain their variations in depth. Understanding the phenomenon is also economically important, because the grenadier is a commercial species whose conservation depends on understanding its genetic diversity.

twice; thus, it was probably present in the last common ancestor of tetrapods and lobe-finned fish. It is also present in today's "walking" fish, including little skates, lungfish, and blind cavefish. It apparently developed at least 420 MYA, long before any group left the water.

Perhaps even more fascinating is that some present-day fish are still evolving to leave the water. These include blennies in the South Pacific and wall-climbing catfish in Ecuador.

RAPID FISH EVOLUTION

One of the most important discoveries in fish evolution is the speed at which fish can evolve. Evolution has always been assumed to occur over geological time. Scientists believed that people could not actually see evolution occurring in organisms with relatively long life cycles, like fish. But recent studies show that fish can evolve extremely rapidly.

The Guppy Project, which began in 2007, builds on the many studies of Trinidadian guppies dating back to 1990. These studies followed guppies in nature living with and without predators. Past research tested predictions based on evolutionary theory and measured rates of evolution in nature. The Guppy Project grew out of a key finding of this research, as stated on the project's web page: "Evolution is tens of thousands of times faster than had been perceived in the fossil record."[5]

Guppy Project scientists, including David Reznick, Joe Travis, Ron Bassar, and Tim Coulson, are now exploring the consequences of this rapid evolution. In the past, evolutionary processes have been assumed to occur so slowly that they could be ignored when studying ecological processes. The guppy studies are based on a new approach, the eco-evo theory, in which scientists assume evolution interacts with ecology. The scientists are quantifying these interactions and looking at how they affect ecosystems. For example, researchers have shown that large populations of guppies cause environmental changes. These changes then cause guppies to evolve as the altered environment selects for different individuals in their populations.

Fish are also evolving rapidly in Africa's Congo River, particularly the Lower Congo, below the city of Kinshasa. This 220-mile (350 km) stretch of the river supports 320 fish species, compared to only 115 species along the entire Upper Nile River, a distance of 870 miles (1,400 km).[6] Two scientists at the American Museum of Natural History (AMNH), Melanie Stiassny and Bob Schelly, are trying to figure out what environmental factors are driving the evolution of this incredible diversity.

Stiassny and Schelly realized that answers to their questions must be hidden in the depths of the river. They collaborated with other scientists to map the riverbed using sonar, or echo sounding. Among other things, the results showed that the Congo is the world's deepest river. It reaches 722 feet (220 m) deep in one place. According to Stiassny, "It's almost like you're boating over a mountain range. There are huge peaks and tremendous troughs."[7]

Currents in the Lower Congo are wild and variable. Deeps, shallows, and underwater structures make many different habitats. This incredible underwater diversity drives fish evolution. For example, two distinct populations of the species *Teleogramma brichardi* live on opposite sides of the river. The populations look very similar, but DNA analyses show DNA differences of 5 percent. This is a very large difference; chimpanzee and human DNA varies by only 1.2 percent.[8] This difference indicates that the fish populations are not

The Congo River is home to nearly 900 species of fish. Of these, 80 percent are found in no other lake or river.[9]

interbreeding—mutations in one population are not being passed to the other. Thus, rapid evolution is occurring, and the populations are separating into two new species.

HUMAN IMPACTS ON FISH EVOLUTION

Another key discovery in fish evolution is the impact of humans. Evolution occurs most rapidly when environmental stress is greatest. Climate change, for example, is having dramatic effects.

The spawning times of Alaska pink salmon, *Oncorhynchus gorbuscha*, are changing in response to climate change. According to a 2012 University of Alaska study, warming stream temperatures are causing salmon to migrate to the ocean two weeks earlier than they did 40 years ago. Over 17 generations, numbers of late-migrating salmon decreased by 20 percent. There were obvious genetic changes in offspring from the highest-temperature years of the study. According to author David Tallmon, these results offer evidence that salmon can adapt to climate change. However, this adaptation also decreases genetic variation. "We may exhaust the ability of these wild populations to adapt," says Tallmon. This would decrease their ability to respond to future environmental changes.[10]

Fish evolution is currently a vital and flourishing science. It is much better understood than it was just a few decades ago, and every day brings more information. Two important lessons from recent studies in fish evolution transcend the world of fish and apply to

CLIMATE CHANGE AND HERRING

Rising carbon dioxide levels are a major cause of climate change. When carbon dioxide dissolves in the oceans, it becomes carbonic acid and increases the acidity of the ocean. Most fish larvae do not survive well at higher acidities, but herring are an exception. In one study, their survival was 20 percent higher than at lower acidity.[11] Scientists think this is partly because they normally spawn near the ocean floor, where carbon dioxide levels are higher, so they are already adapted. Also, higher carbon dioxide levels affect food webs. Algae and zooplankton populations grow larger, providing more food for herring.

Over the last 530 million years, fish have evolved to include more than 34,800 known species on the planet.[12]

evolution in general. First, evolution is not always a long, slow process. Sometimes it happens very rapidly. Second, evolution is not a process that occurred in the past and stopped. It is ongoing, very active, and continuing all around us.

ESSENTIAL FACTS

PERIOD TIMELINE

CAMBRIAN	ORDOVICIAN	SILURIAN	DEVONIAN	CARBONIFEROUS	PERMIAN
541–485.4 million years ago (MYA)	485.4–443.8 MYA	443.8–419.2 MYA	419.2–358.9 MYA	358.9–298.9 MYA	298.9–251.9 MYA
Metaspriggina		*Andreolepis hedei* *Lophosteus superbus*	*Gogoselachus lynbeazleyae* *Tiktaalik roseae*		

NUMBER OF SPECIES

There are approximately 33,421 species of bony fish, another 1,259 species of cartilaginous fish, 127 species of jawless fish, and eight species of lobe-finned fish.

IMPORTANT ANIMALS AND SPECIMENS

- *Metaspriggina* (518 MYA), a fossil fish found in Canada's Burgess Shale, may be the first chordate, the ancestor of all modern chordates and vertebrates.
- *Tiktaalik roseae* (375 MYA), a fossil discovered on Ellesmere Island, Canada, in 2006, is a "fishapod," representing a transitional form between lobe-finned fish and tetrapods.
- Cichlids (present day), a group of percomorphs, have undergone a massive radiation in East Africa's Lake Victoria and surrounding lakes, evolving more than 700 closely related species.
- *Oncorhynchus gorbuscha* (present day), the pink salmon, is evolving in response to climate change by migrating upstream earlier to avoid higher temperatures.

					Latimeria chalumnae Bichirs Gars and bowfins *Synodontis multipunctatus* Cichlids *Oncorhynchus gorbuscha*
251.9–201.3 MYA	201.3–145 MYA	145–66 MYA	66–23 MYA	23–2.6 MYA	2.6 MYA–present
TRIASSIC	JURASSIC	CRETACEOUS	PALEOGENE	NEOGENE	QUATERNARY

IMPORTANT SCIENTISTS

- J. L. B. Smith named and described the first specimen of the coelacanth *Latimeria chalumnae*, discovered in 1938.
- Neil Shubin of the University of Chicago led the team that discovered *Tiktaalik roseae*, an important transition fossil between fish and tetrapods.
- Terry Ord and Georgina Cooke of Australia's University of New South Wales identified 33 families of fish that independently moved from water to land.
- Paleontologist Jenny Clack discovered an early Devonian species of *Acanthostega* that had fins with tiny fingers, showing that fingers developed long before fish left the water.

QUOTE

"Evolutionary change doesn't always take thousands of years."

—Mark Christie, Oregon State University researcher

adaptive radiation
An evolutionary process in which organisms diversify rapidly from a common ancestor into a huge number of new species.

arthropod
An invertebrate animal of the large phylum Arthropoda, which includes insects, spiders, and crustaceans.

batoids
All species of skates and rays, members of class Chondrichthyes, subclass Elasmobranchii; they are flattened, diamond-shaped animals.

cartilage
An often translucent tissue that is firm but elastic.

clade
A group of species that all descended from a common ancestor.

cladogram
A diagram showing how different species and groups relate to one another.

climate change
A process affecting the planet that is causing temperatures around the world to rise.

convergent evolution
An evolutionary process in which two groups of organisms evolve similar characteristics, even though they are not closely related and may live in different locations.

gene
A unit of hereditary information found in a chromosome.

gnathostomes
Jawed vertebrates, or members of superclass Gnathostomata, which comprise more than 99 percent of all vertebrates.

lineage
The sequence of descent from an ancestor.

morphology
The branch of biology that deals with the form of living organisms and the relationships between their structures.

niche
A species' interaction with its habitat, such as what it feeds on, what feeds on it, and the role it plays in its ecological community.

notochord
A flexible rod extending the length of the body of certain organisms.

phylogeny
The evolutionary history of a species or group of organisms.

tetrapod
An animal that evolved from an ancestor that had two sets of limbs; amphibians, mammals, and reptiles are all tetrapods.

transitional fossil
A fossil that appears to be an intermediate stage, having characteristics of both an ancestral form and a more modern form.

ADDITIONAL RESOURCES

SELECTED BIBLIOGRAPHY

"Article: Fish Evolution Takes a Wild Ride." *American Museum of Natural History*, Dec. 2009, amnh.org. Accessed 20 May 2018.

Fricke, Ron, William Eschmeyer, and Jon David Fong. "Species by Family/Subfamily in the Catalog of Fishes." *California Academy of Sciences*, 4 Sept. 2018, calacademy.org. Accessed 10 Sept. 2018.

Zimmer, Carl. "Evolution's Baby Steps." *National Geographic*, 27 Aug. 2014. nationalgeographic.com. Accessed 7 Aug. 2018.

FURTHER READINGS

Clark, Robert. *Evolution: A Visual Record*. Phaidon, 2016.

Gurr, Brenda. *Monster Sharks: Megalodon and Other Giant Prehistoric Predators of the Deep*. becker&mayer! kids, 2018.

Hand, Carol. *Bringing Back Our Oceans*. Abdo, 2017.

Nickum, Mary Jo. *Coelacanth: The Greatest Fish Story Ever Told*. Aquitaine, 2016.

ONLINE RESOURCES

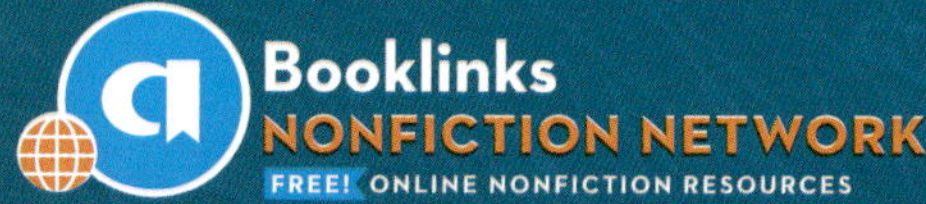

To learn more about the evolution of fish, visit **abdobooklinks.com**. These links are routinely monitored and updated to provide the most current information available.

MORE INFORMATION

For more information on this subject, contact or visit the following organizations:

AMERICAN SOCIETY OF ICHTHYOLOGISTS AND HERPETOLOGISTS (ASIH)

PO Box 1897
Lawrence, KS 66044-8897
800-627-0326 ext. 405

The ASIH is an international organization devoted to the study of fish, reptiles, and amphibians. It communicates new information and supports young scientists in these fields.

NATIONAL MARINE FISHERIES SERVICE (NMFS)

1315 East-West Highway
Silver Spring, MD 20910
301-427-8000

The NMFS is a government agency responsible for management of US marine resources, including fish. It regulates ocean fishing and manages marine life and habitats near US shores.

SOCIETY OF VERTEBRATE PALEONTOLOGY (SVP)

9650 Rockville Pike
Bethesda, MD 20814
301-634-7024
vertpaleo.org/Home.aspx

SVP is a nonprofit organization for scientists, students, and others interested in vertebrate paleontology science and education. It shares information among members and supports discovery, conservation, and protection of both vertebrate fossils and fossil sites.

SOURCE NOTES

CHAPTER 1. FROM FISH TO TETRAPODS

1. John Long. "The Oldest Fish in the World Lived 500 Million Years Ago." *The Conversation*, 11 June 2014, theconversation.com. Accessed 15 May 2018.

2. "Burgess Shale. *Anomalocaris canadensis* (proto-arthropod)." *Smithsonian National Museum of Natural History*, n.d., si.edu. Accessed 15 Apr. 2018.

3. Long, "The Oldest Fish in the World."

4. Ron Fricke, William Eschmeyer, and Jon David Fong. "Species by Family/Subfamily in the Catalog of Fishes." *California Academy of Sciences*, 4 Sept. 2018, calacademy.org. Accessed 10 Sept. 2018.

5. Fricke, Eschmeyer, and Fong, "Species by Family/Subfamily in the Catalog of Fishes."

CHAPTER 2. HAGFISH AND LAMPREYS

1. Ron Fricke, William Eschmeyer, and Jon David Fong. "Species by Family/Subfamily in the Catalog of Fishes." *California Academy of Sciences*, 4 Sept. 2018, calacademy.org. Accessed 10 Sept. 2018.

2. Hannah Waters. "14 Fun Facts About Hagfish." *Smithsonian.com*, 17 Oct. 2012, smithsonian.com. Accessed 15 Apr. 2018.

3. Fricke, Eschmeyer, and Fong, "Species by Family/Subfamily in the Catalog of Fishes."

4. Bob Strauss. "500 Million Years of Fish Evolution." *ThoughtCo.*, 20 Apr. 2017, thoughtco.com. Accessed 15 May 2018.

5. Bob Strauss. "Haikouichthys." *ThoughtCo.*, 17 Mar. 2017, thoughtco.com. Accessed 15 May 2018.

6. Strauss, "500 Million Years of Fish Evolution."

7. Strauss, "500 Million Years of Fish Evolution."

8. "Ostracoderms—An Extinct Group with Heavy Armour." *University of the Southern Cape*, 2018, uwc.ac.za. Accessed 25 Apr. 2018.

CHAPTER 3. SHARKS, SKATES, AND RAYS

1. Ron Fricke, William Eschmeyer, and Jon David Fong. "Species by Family/Subfamily in the Catalog of Fishes." *California Academy of Sciences*, 4 Sept. 2018, calacademy.org. Accessed 10 Sept. 2018.

2. Fricke, Eschmeyer, and Fong, "Species by Family/Subfamily in the Catalog of Fishes."

3. Martin Brazeau and Matt Friedman. "The Origin and Early Phylogenetic History of Jawed Vertebrates." *Nature*, 23 Apr. 2015, nature.com. Accessed 15 Apr. 2018.

4. "Sharks." *Smithsonian National Museum of Natural History*, 2017, si.edu. Accessed 15 Apr. 2018.

5. Fricke, Eschmeyer, and Fong, "Species by Family/Subfamily in the Catalog of Fishes."

6. Fricke, Eschmeyer, and Fong, "Species by Family/Subfamily in the Catalog of Fishes."

7. Fricke, Eschmeyer, and Fong, "Species by Family/Subfamily in the Catalog of Fishes."

8. Stuart Gary. "Fossil Ancestor Suggests Sharks Once Had Bony Skeletons." *ABC Science*, 29 May 2015, abc.net. Accessed 15 Apr. 2018.

CHAPTER 4. LOBE-FINNED FISH AND TETRAPODS

1. "Sarcopterygii—Lobe-Finned Fishes." *University College London*, n.d., ucl.ac.uk. Accessed 12 Apr. 2018.

2. "Coelacanths." *National Geographic*, 2018, nationalgeographic.com. Accessed 6 May 2018.

3. Ron Fricke, William Eschmeyer, and Jon David Fong. "Species by Family/Subfamily in the Catalog of Fishes." *California Academy of Sciences*, 4 Sept. 2018, calacademy.org. Accessed 10 Sept. 2018.

4. Patrick Monahan. "Fish May Have Evolved to Live on Land More Than 30 Times." *Science*, 16 June 2016, sciencemag.org. Accessed 15 Apr. 2018.

5. Mary Caperton Morton. "Evolution of Eyes, Not Limbs, Led Fish onto Land." *Earth Magazine*, 28 June 2017, earthmagazine.org. Accessed 15 Apr. 2018.

CHAPTER 5. THE FIRST BONY FISH

1. Ron Fricke, William Eschmeyer, and Jon David Fong. "Species by Family/Subfamily in the Catalog of Fishes." *California Academy of Sciences*, 4 Sept. 2018, calacademy.org. Accessed 10 Sept. 2018.

2. "Devonian Period." *National Geographic*, 2018, nationalgeograpic.com. Accessed 9 May 2018.

3. John Roach. "Jaws, Teeth of Earliest Bony Fish Discovered." *National Geographic News*, 1 Aug. 2007, nationalgeographic.com. Accessed 15 May 2018.

4. Bob Strauss. "500 Million Years of Fish Evolution." *ThoughtCo.*, 20 Apr. 2017, thoughtco.com. Accessed 15 May 2018.

5. "Blue Whale." *National Geographic*, 2018, nationalgeographic.com. Accessed 7 May 2018.

6. Strauss, "500 Million Years of Fish Evolution."

7. Bob Strauss. "Xiphactinus." *ThoughtCo.*, 7 Mar. 2017, thoughtco.com. Accessed 15 May 2018.

8. Michael Rogers. "The Ten Largest Sharks in History." *Shark Sider*, 29 June 2016, sharksider.com. Accessed 20 Apr. 2018.

9. Rogers, "The Ten Largest Sharks in History."

CHAPTER 6. MODERN ORDERS OF BONY FISH

1. Ron Fricke, William Eschmeyer, and Jon David Fong. "Species by Family/Subfamily in the Catalog of Fishes." *California Academy of Sciences*, 4 Sept. 2018, calacademy.org. Accessed 10 Sept. 2018.

2. Fricke, Eschmeyer, and Fong, "Species by Family/Subfamily in the Catalog of Fishes."

3. Carl Zimmer. "Evolution's Baby Steps." *National Geographic*, 27 Aug. 2014, nationalgeographic.com. Accessed 15 May 2018.

4. Zimmer, "Evolution's Baby Steps."

5. Fricke, Eschmeyer, and Fong, "Species by Family/Subfamily in the Catalog of Fishes."

6. "Acipenseriformes (Sturgeons and Paddlefishes)." *Encyclopedia.com*, n.d., encyclopedia.com. Accessed 12 May 2018.

7. "Evolutionary History. Interview with Jack Horner, Paleontologist, Museum of the Rockies, Bozeman, MT." *Pallid Sturgeon Recovery Program*, 2013, pallidsturgeon.org. Accessed 20 Apr. 2018.

8. "Sturgeon More Critically Endangered Than Any Other Group of Species." *International Union for Conservation of Nature*, 18 Mar. 2018, iucn.org. Accessed 20 May 2018.

9. "Sturgeon More Critically Endangered Than Any Other Group of Species."

10. "Gar." *National Geographic*, 2015–2018, nationalgeographic.com. Accessed 13 May 2018.

11. "Actinopterygii: Ray-Finned Fishes." *University College London*, n.d., ucl.ac.uk. Accessed 13 Apr. 2018.

CHAPTER 7. EARLY TELEOST GROUPS

1. Ron Fricke, William Eschmeyer, and Jon David Fong. "Species by Family/Subfamily in the Catalog of Fishes." *California Academy of Sciences*, 4 Sept. 2018, calacademy.org. Accessed 10 Sept. 2018.

2. Ricardo Betancur-R et al. "The Tree of Life and a New Classification of Bony Fishes." *PLOS Currents Tree of Life*, 18 Apr. 2013, plos.org. Accessed 20 May 2018.

3. Betancur-R et al, "The Tree of Life and a New Classification of Bony Fishes."

4. Nick Stockton. "How Evolution Gave Some Fish Their Electric Powers." *Wired*, 28 Aug. 2014, wired.com. Accessed 20 May 2018.

5. Stockton, "How Evolution Gave Some Fish Their Electric Powers."

6. Dave Cooper Campbell. "The Evolution of Body Size in the Order Siluriformes." *University of Southern Mississippi*, Honor Thesis, No. 321, 2015, usm.edu. Accessed 20 May 2018.

7. University of Michigan. "Killer Catfish? Venomous Species Surprisingly Common, Study Finds." *ScienceDaily*, 15 Dec. 2009, sciencedaily.com. Accessed 20 May 2018.

8. Fricke, Eschmeyer, and Fong, "Species by Family/Subfamily in the Catalog of Fishes."

9. "Shrinking Salmon." *Evolution Library*, 2001, pbs.org. Accessed 20 May 2018.

10. "High-Speed Evolution: Study Shows Salmon Can Change Their Genes in a Single Generation." *Daily Mail*, 19 Dec. 2011, dailymail.co.uk. Accessed 20 May 2018.

CHAPTER 8. THE PERCOMORPH CLADE

1. "Actinopterygii: Ray-Finned Fishes." *University College London*, n.d., ucl.ac.uk. Accessed 7 May 13, 2018.

2. Bjorn Carey. "Cichlid Fish Genome Helps Tell Story of Adaptive Evolution, Stanford Scientists Say." *Stanford Report*, 22 Sept. 2014, stanford.edu. Accessed 25 May 2018.

3. University of Wyoming. "Scientists Solve Fish Evolution Mystery." *Phys.org*, 10 Feb. 2017, phys.org. Accessed 20 May 2018.

4. Laura Spinney. "The Little Fish Fight Back." *Guardian*, 3 Aug. 2005, theguardian.com. Accessed 25 May 2018.

5. Christopher Foote. "How the Flatfish Arose in the Blink of an Evolutionary Eye." *BMC Series Blog*, 24 Oct. 2016, blogs.biomedcentral.com. Accessed 25 May 2018.

6. Gina Kolata. "A Breakthrough on Evolution as Guppies Change Behavior." *New York Times*, 26 July 1990, nytimes.com. Accessed 20 May 2018.

CHAPTER 9. FISH EVOLUTION TODAY

1. Katherine Unger Baillie. "Today's Most Successful Fish Weren't Always Evolutionary Standouts." *Phys.org*, 27 Sept. 2016, phys.org. Accessed 25 May 2018.

2. Alice Klein. "These Fish Are Evolving Right Now to Become Land-Dwellers." *New Scientist*, 16 Mar. 2017, newscientist.com. Accessed 15 May 2018.

3. University of Central Florida. "Fish's Super Power May Offer Clues About Biodiversity Evolution." *UCF Today*, n.d., ucf.edu. Accessed 14 Apr. 2018.

4. University of Central Florida, "Fish's Super Power."

5. "How Do Ecological and Evolutionary Processes Interact in Nature?" *Guppy Project*, n.d., theguppyproject.weebly.com. Accessed 22 May 2018.

6. "Article: Fish Evolution Takes a Wild Ride." *American Museum of Natural History*, Dec. 2009, amnh.org. Accessed 20 May 2018.

7. "Article: Fish Evolution Takes a Wild Ride."

8. "Article: Fish Evolution Takes a Wild Ride."

9. "Fish of the Congo River." *World Wildlife Fund*, n.d., wwf.panda.org. Accessed 20 May 2018.

10. Mollie Bloudoff-Indelicato. "Salmon Evolve to Cope with Climate Change." *Scientific American*, 13 July 2012, scientificamerican.com. Accessed 20 May 2018.

11. Helmholtz Association of German Research Centres. "Ocean Acidification: Herring Could Benefit from an Altered Food Chain." *Phys.org*, 20 Mar. 2018, phys.org. Accessed 13 Sept. 2018.

12. Bob Strauss. "500 Million Years of Fish Evolution." *ThoughtCo.*, 20 Apr. 2017, thoughtco.com. Accessed 15 May 2018.

INDEX

ABOUT THE AUTHOR

Carol Hand has a PhD in zoology from the University of Georgia. She has taught college biology, written biology assessments for national assessment companies, and written high school science curricula for a national company. For the past nine years, she has been a freelance science writer. She has authored more than 50 young adult science books, including biology titles such as *Introduction to Genetics*, *Reviving Extinct Species*, *Bringing Back Our Oceans*, and *Climate Change: Our Warming Earth*.